THE DISRESPECT AGENDA

THE DISRESPECT AGENDA

OR HOW THE WRONG KIND OF NICENESS IS MAKING US WEAK AND UNHAPPY

Lincoln Allison

THE
SOCIAL
AFFAIRS
UNIT

British Library Cataloguing in Publication Data
A catalogue record of this book is available from the British Library

Printed and bound in the United Kingdom

ISBN-13: 978-1-904863-30-4

Social Affairs Unit
314–322 Regent Street
London W1B 5SA
www.socialaffairsunit.org.uk

CONTENTS

PROLEGOMENON:
SCENES OF RESPECT AND DISRESPECT

Another characteristic, which seems to belong to the
nation without distinction of class, is a commonsense
prudence and practicality which readily surrenders 'the
point of honour' to utility. A story of the Duke of
Wellington during the Peninsular War is a good
illustration. He had planned a combined operation on a
large scale, and called on the Spanish General to secure
his co-operation. That hidalgo replied that it was not
consistent with his dignity to grant a request from the
English commander unless he went down on his knees
to ask for it. The Duke explained afterwards that he had
wanted the thing done and did not care a twopenny
damn about going on his knees; 'so down I plumped'.
No French or German General would have abased his
dignity in this way, and presumably the operation would
have been given up.[1]

The following pages contain a few of the incidents that suggested to me the concept of respect (and the need people feel
to be respected) as a worthy topic of investigation.

⟶≈≈⟵

I am in the lobby of a small hotel in Nicosia, waiting for a
travel company employee to come back to me with details of
an excursion. The only other person in the vicinity is small,
moustachioed, pot-bellied and, unlike most of the people in
the hotel, about my age. He correctly assumes that we are
attending different branches of the same conference, and

strikes up a conversation in an accent which is, to my ear, unspecifically American. How do I find the hotel? And the transport to the conference venue? His interest in my answers is somewhere between minimal and non-existent. Things here are not up to his usual standard. Actually, his attendance here is part of a trip round the world, and he is hoping for much better treatment in Singapore and Hong Kong. His tone and 'body language' reveal that, as Wodehouse would put it, he is far from gruntled.

Now we get to the serious stuff. How do I find the other people in my workshop? Scarcely pretending to listen to the answer, he goes on to reveal that he has had a rather shocking experience. Yesterday was his presentation, and the young Italian woman who had been allocated the task of responding to it had been *disrespectful*. Of course, he would defend with his life her rights to *criticise* or to *disagree*, but he is a quantitative social scientist with a global reputation, and criticism and disagreement should be expressed *respectfully*.

If he had thought that, just because I, too, have grey hair, I am going to be sympathetic to his plight, he has made a big mistake. 'What form,' I demand, 'should her respect take?' Is she supposed to say that he is really distinguished and they are all grateful for his contribution to knowledge, but might there not be a tiny, weeny point on page 17 that is ever such a little bit wrong from a certain point of view?

I go on to tell him that, in my opinion, 95 – no 98 – per cent of material produced by social scientists who imagine they have global reputations is complete rubbish, utterly misconceived from start to finish, and that the chances of his work (which, of course, I have never read) being in the remaining 2 per cent are drastically reduced not only by his self-ascribed 'quantitative' status, but also by his need for respect. What academic debate needs – if it is to be worth anything at all – is a good deal less respect and much more of the pure, fresh ordure of scorn. If he really believes he has something true and interesting to say, then he should welcome disrespect. Debate should not be politely couched on the notion that we are all right in our own way; it should not be held within 'appropriate' boundaries; it should be free, and based on the assumption that genuine intellectual achievement is very rare indeed.

Actually, I don't say any of this – or hardly any. It is too early in the morning. I mutter something about respect being an overstated virtue in the academic world, make my excuses and leave, thus depriving myself of my excursion information for the time being. Would the world be a better place if I had spoken freely?

—∿∿—

There is another American professor (I promise this will be the last) who is an official visitor to our department. He is a large man whose personal style aims at gravitas, though he is not without personal warmth. He would love to see an English 'soccer' game, he has said – several times. So, late one autumn afternoon, we hatch a plan to go that night to a game in Walsall. Our wives have been duly phoned. 'We' are myself, the professor, a colleague and a graduate student. Unfortunately, our only form of transport is the graduate student's Mini, and three of us are over six feet tall. But we cram in. Also, it has hardly any petrol, so we must now go to a garage. The weather is becoming squally, with the rain varying its trajectory from the vertical to the horizontal.

All the way to the garage, the professor talks. He tells us about his period as chairman of his department back home, and about his membership of the council of the university and the size of the university's budget that he has to review. He is even kind enough to tell us that he owns a good deal of land, more than anyone else in the department, and an amount exceeded by only one member of the council. As the graduate student goes to fill his tank with petrol, there is a pause. 'So – to sum up,' says my colleague, 'over there, you're a bigshot, whereas right now you're just a fat man in the back of a Mini going to Walsall in the rain.'

Any possibility of friendship depends on his response...

—∿∿—

9

I am sitting in my office at the university, doing whatever it is academics do on quiet afternoons – or pretending to, anyway. To my relief (I am bored), there is a knock on the door. It is barely a knock, not much more than a scratching, really. 'Come in,' I shout, and Mihoko slips into the room, opening the door only just enough for her slender frame to get through. Head bowed, she makes her way toward my desk with that distinctively Japanese shuffle I think of as the 'geisha girl walk', muttering apologies about disturbing me. I want to tell her to stand up straight and not to apologise, because somebody, presumably her father, is paying good money for my services.

As it happens, I have a good deal of respect for Mihoko's intelligence and determination. She is one of our first Japanese undergraduates, and when I met her three days after she arrived in England, I thought it was a hopeless case, that her poor English would prevent her from making much progress. But she is now in her final year, and she can write a well-constructed, intelligent essay in English. I am her 'personal tutor' and I also teach her, and I am proud of her progress, finding it unimaginable that I would have thrown myself into a Japanese university at her age. But she cannot argue, cannot assert herself, can barely contribute to discussion. I have a kind of dream, that one day she will look me in the eye and say: 'You're talking bollocks, Lincoln.' But the burden of respect is too heavy. She is not going to do this inside three years as an undergraduate. Probably not in three decades. Does 'assertiveness training' really work?

'Once proud.' 'Once mighty.' *Twice* champions of England (in the 1920s and the 1960s). That is how my little football team is always described, whenever it gets further than the local news – by being promoted or relegated or by being drawn against some famous club in a cup competition. But here we are, on one of those grey afternoons that always bring to mind the witticism that England has 25 weeks of autumn and 25 weeks of spring. We are away to Oxford, at the grotty little Manor Ground, and we are standing behind the goal, some 2,000 of us. Oxford, a place for which I reserve the most cheerful of contempt, having been an undergraduate and a postgraduate there, and having had my first non-manual job there. Oxford, which, at the time of our last and well-remembered mightiness, was called Headington United, and played in something called the Southern League. But we have fallen, Oxford has risen, and now we meet in the Third Division.

We are not doing too badly. Admittedly, we are 0–1 down, having given away a goal in the first few minutes. But now, with 20 minutes to go, we are the better team, pressing strongly and getting increasingly close to an equaliser. Then, perhaps slightly strangely for a team 1–0 up, Oxford bring on as substitute a big, blond, 'old-fashioned' centre-forward. Shortly before he scores, an astute young man to my right points out that nobody is marking him. When he scores his third goal (having been on the field for all of 11 minutes), I judge the distance between him and the nearest defender to be 12 yards when he receives the ball. The trouble is, our manager has only been in the job ten days and has no qualifications for it; he has just demonstrated the greatest degree of tactical incompetence I have seen in 40 years of playing and watching football.

As the defenders react with that curious body language of despair and incomprehension that follows conceding a goal – some sitting down, one lashing the ball furiously back into the net and others urging greater efforts – the Oxford United fans raise a chorus of 'You're Shit and You Know You Are'. This is sung to the tune of Go West by the Pet Shop Boys and is supposedly a 'gay' anthem. And we, all 2,000 of us, bellow back: 'We're Shit and We Know We Are' at five times their volume. The grins are enormous, the sense of shared happiness affects everyone. We have just broken the iron, if unwritten, rule that football fans never give an inch, always trade insult for insult, aggression for aggression. We have achieved something akin to the logical structure of Buddhism, a kind of self-respect that consists entirely of not needing self-respect.

The whole ritual, in later years, becomes hackneyed, but that does not undermine the original insight.

———∿∿∿———

It is still in the days when we interview candidates for undergraduate places, keen to seek out individuals whose ability is greater than their formal qualifications would suggest. For this is still an aspiring university, and the applications for 'Philosophy and Politics' are by no means as numerous as we would wish. We have just interviewed a tough-looking young guy from what we know to be an authoritarian public school in which beating and compulsory military activity play a part. We liked him: he had clear answers to questions; some of them were obviously wrong, but he had a good instinct for when to retreat and when to face us down. The interview ended in comradely fashion, with smiles and handshakes.

Now we have another young man, slimmer and more handsome than the last, from a well-known progressive school. He has, it says on his application form, been taught to think for himself and to care for others (yes, both of those things at once). But he seems irritatingly anxious to please, and if we press him on an answer, he simply agrees with us. He leaves in an atmosphere of dissatisfaction tinged with bewilderment. Our underlying criterion, as we always assure each other, is to find people we would enjoy teaching, and this has been a poor afternoon – only three out of eight, and only one of those likely to come.

'Why is it,' asks the professor of philosophy, 'that if you educate people by telling them that they are individuals and must express themselves, you end up with boring conformists, but if you beat the living daylights out of them you might just produce an individual?'

———∿∿∿———

This is an exciting journey – to say the least. The last town we came through was entirely deserted, blasted and blackened, having been the epicentre of recent hostilities. And now – particularly interesting for a political theorist – we are beyond the boundaries of anything that might reasonably be called a state. *What* a lively example for my first-year lectures: nobody in these parts is upholding, to any degree, the claim to a monopoly right over physical violence, to use the Weberian terminology.

We are in the foothills of the Caucasus mountains, my friend and I. The car is a Lada, the road is appalling. I don't know how the Soviet Union built its roads, but they are a long way below Roman standards. Once there is a hole in the tarmac, the water pours down it and it becomes a pit. We have looked down into potholes that are eight feet deep; the driving has to be very careful.

And as we come round a bend, we find a vehicle blocking the road – conveniently parked where the road is on a ledge, so that it offers a sheer mountainside to the right and a long drop to the left. A Land Rover Discovery! This brand of vehicle is the gangster's transport of choice in these parts. But even if it wasn't, Dr Watson would hardly struggle to diagnose the situation. Of the four men leaning against it, 100 per cent are wearing leather jackets and 75 per cent black caps; 50 per cent are carrying semi-automatic weapons. So far as I am concerned, they may as well be wearing those old eyemasks and red and black T-shirts, and be carrying bags labelled 'swag'.

Sasha takes the initiative, stops the car and greets them firmly but politely. He talks in Megrelian, which he understands because his wife is one of those blue-eyed, blonde Megrelians who are something of a DNA phenomenon in these parts. I guess he says 'What's the problem?' or something along those lines, and when they reply, he introduces me ('*Angliyski*' comes into it somewhere). So we all shake hands and I practise method-acting as a calm and friendly persona. It is a risk, but in these parts 'the guest is sent by God' and there is a code.

The bottom line is that I am not kidnapped and we are not comprehensively robbed, but most of our petrol is siphoned off 'for the war effort'. ('Which fucking war?' I think, since there are, arguably, four going on within a medium distance of here.

And does the Lada's fuel really work in the Discovery?) But one is strangely polite in these circumstances. Respectful, even. And so are they quite respectful, though the loss of petrol is serious and nearly results in my not getting home.

———∞∞∞———

I am in Melbourne, in a pub. My presence here is due to a complicated arrangement involving academic fellowships, and I know nobody in this city. But it has been fixed for me to meet a friend of a friend of a friend in this pub at this time, with a view to watching an Australian Rules football match. So I ask the barmaid whether she knows somebody called Dinny who might be present.

'Hey, Dinny,' she shouts, continuing to attend to her duties. 'There's a Pom wants you.'

He is a stout, middle-aged man wearing a shirt with a variety of interesting stains on it.

'Jeez,' he shouts back (or something like that). 'What a sorry-looking specimen. Give him a beer.'

I am beginning to think I might like it here.

———∞∞∞———

When it rains on Sunday afternoons, the local corner shop, which is run by a family of Punjabi origin whom I have known for many years, does particularly good trade. On this occasion, young Hari has been left in charge. He has spotted something on the discreetly placed CCTV camera that has led to an altercation with a young white man, who is tattooed, ear-ringed and drunk. 'Whad yer wanna look in *my* pockets for?' he demands. 'No fucking respect...that's what it fucking is.' And, having discovered this talismanic word, he uses it again: 'You ought to show some fucking respect.'

I am seething. Speech or pre-emptive strike first? Why on earth would anyone respect you, rat-boy? I cannot imagine anyone less worthy of respect. But neither words nor actions are necessary. Rat-boy has been joined by two companions, one white and one black, who pull him away and remonstrate with him to the effect that Hari is a good bloke and shouldn't be hassled. As they leave, the black lad says to Hari 'Sorry, mate – it's the Stella talking.'

———◁◉▷———

The celebrations of my 60th birthday. After the ascent of Pendle and the football match and the dinner (Lancastrian menu), but before the disco, there is a ceremony. It is to consist of a short speech by my youngest son, a presentation, the singing of 'Happy Birthday' and the cutting of the cake. The presentation is of a cricket ball, mounted on a stand; it is the ball with which, in the later stages of my 60th year, I took a hat-trick. It seems to me the only appropriate presentation, because it symbolises luck. Lucky enough to be still alive and still playing cricket, and (luck *in extremis*) to find three batsmen daft enough to get out to three successive balls.

In his speech, he refers to me as 'the poor old bugger', and describes how this was a game that was more or less lost, in which everybody else had bowled and it was very hot and they didn't want any more damage to their figures, and as I'd bothered to turn up... When he finishes, he has a big grin on his face as he hands me the cricket ball on a nice little stand. The woman next to my wife whispers in her ear: 'Absolutely no respect whatsoever...but a good deal of love.'

PART ONE

THE DEMAND FOR RESPECT

1

STARTING POINTS

This is an essay on ethical and political philosophy, written by an author who is a sceptic, a conservative, a liberal, a utilitarian and a bit of an anarchist, and who will argue that the mental attitudes indicated by these words are necessary to each other, at least in the senses specified.

The easiest of these five conditions to maintain is scepticism. It requires non-belief, reluctance to believe without good reason, and approval of non-belief in others. The paradox – that it is a condition of belief in non-belief – should not worry anyone. The opposite of scepticism – a generalised approval of belief *per se* – does not have a particular name in English; it might be called 'credibilism' or 'credulism' (which would have slightly more hostile connotations). But the phenomenon certainly exists, and I will be quoting the actor and writer Peter Ustinov, Prince Charles and governments in general as being credulists. In summarising the nature of scepticism, it is useful to recall Bertrand Russell's reply when he shocked a member of his audience by rejecting both Christianity and Marxism. The questioner appeared to believe that one had to accept one or the other, and had accused Russell of not believing anything. The reply was 'I believe today is Tuesday.'

The least meaningful of the labels would appear to be liberalism. At the time of writing, in France and the USA it is taken to refer to almost exactly opposite beliefs. In France, where few people would describe themselves as liberals, it is taken to refer to a belief in the primacy of individual self-interest, the necessity of capitalist markets and the acceptance of 'globalisation'. Liberalism in this sense must, by definition, be opposed to socialism, even in its moderate 19th-century sense of indicating only a general belief in social solidarity and progress. In America, by contrast, although being a 'liberal' may suggest a disapproval of government regulation of sexual practices, the principal implication is of a greater belief in government than is held by most non-liberals. American 'liberalism', in its popular sense, is descended from the 'New Liberalism' of the late 19th century, which allowed a much greater role for the state in benefiting people and liberating them from the conditions that might be thought to be limiting them. Despite these contradictory usages, I think it still makes a broad kind of sense to call yourself a liberal if you believe that people should choose, as far as possible, the direction of their lives, and should assume responsibility for their choices. Mine is not a 'fundamentalist' liberalism like that of John Locke in the 17th century or Robert Nozick in the 20th: I am not assuming that human beings are bundles of inalienable rights that ought never to be breached. Rather, mine is a consequentialist liberalism, like that of John Stuart Mill, which makes the judgement that the world works better if what happens is left more to individual projects and responsibilities.

'Works better' is a utilitarian term, and utilitarianism is the most important of the five conditions, because the others are justified in its terms. It is also the most complex, and I will offer only a brief summary of what I have written elsewhere on the subject. Utilitarianism is not offered here as having the bogus precision of Jeremy Bentham's 'felicific calculus', but nor is it a moral doctrine so vague and all-embracing that it can be used to justify anything, as its detractors often suggest. Certainly, there are different forms of utilitarianism, and no guarantee that two utilitarians faced with the same choice will come to the same conclusion; but those reservations are true of all ethical persuasions. In general, utilitarianism has three defining conditions (individually necessary, collectively sufficient):

1. It justifies actions according to their consequences and not according to their conformity to pre-existing rules.

2. It attempts to assess those consequences in terms of the aggregate well-being of a relevant population.
3. It construes that well-being sensually, in terms of feelings. Thus, it must have a language of feelings – of pleasure, pain, happiness, misery, etc. – however inadequate that language may be.

Two important and unique logical features of utilitarianism are its *reductionism* and its *aggregationism*: it must always ask for 'bottom line' estimates of who gains and who loses from a policy, and by how much; and it becomes increasingly irrefutable the larger the scale of the decision. What other moral doctrine would even be relevant to the decision of whether to drop an atomic bomb on Hiroshima?

Conservatism poses the most difficult 'membership' problem in the list. Conservatism is generally said to have come into existence as opposition to the 18th-century 'Enlightenment' and the French Revolution of 1789. It typically defends existing practices and institutions against projects that seek to redesign society according to universal (and often newly discovered) principles. It is often the case that conservative sentiments might be expressed by thinkers who could not possibly be described as conservatives in general, such as Edmund Burke or George Orwell. It should also be noted that self-ascribed political 'Conservatism' is relatively rare and largely confined to a handful of English-speaking countries. Although it is quite possible to be a conservative without being a utilitarian, conservative argument is often utilitarian in nature, stressing that rapid change leads to unhappiness, and that old institutions often work better than new ones, simply because they are old.

An important implication of this account of conservatism is that there is no reason for conservatives to agree on anything, except their opposition to wholesale change. I have already indicated that conservatives may or may not be utilitarians; they may also disagree on God, free trade (a notorious historical example), capital punishment and a large range of other important issues. In the 20th century, conservatism was made relatively easy by the existence of socialism in the sense of egalitarian *étatisme*: it is difficult to imagine anything ever again uniting conservatives as effectively as did socialism in this sense.

Thus, since the late 20th century, it has been more difficult to define oneself as a conservative: it is as if the opposition has become more devious and divisive, and has a greater capacity to infiltrate conservatism. 'Multiculturalism', 'the preservation of the environment', the European Union – there is no reason to suppose that English Conservatives would agree on these issues, even if we could clarify their meaning. Thus it becomes at least as difficult as it was in the 19th century to be a conservative. A very pessimistic view might be that, in these circumstances, conservatism has no underlying identity at all.

I do not believe this to be the case. I have always argued that conservatism exists in opposition to a generic phenomenon that must be called humanism, which is the elevation of humanity to something like the status of a deity. For humanists, humanity has unarguable metaphysical qualities. There is a slight difference between deity and humanity, in that, by most accounts, we cannot see God at all, whereas we can see humanity in the everyday sense of dirty, unequal, ignoble and oppressed humans. But this difference becomes trivial if we insist, as humanists do, on talking about humanity metaphysically, as being (to take the two most obvious examples) fundamentally equal and in possession of inalienable rights. And the new, post-socialist enemy is humanist in every bad sense. Much of its rhetoric is based on the assumption that equality is an end in itself. This is to be contrasted with the utilitarian reductionism of, for example, John Stuart Mill and Harriet Taylor, who insisted that their proposals for greater equality between men and women in respect of the right to own property should be subjected to the test of whether it would make society as a whole better off. (Shrewd readers will have noted that what I earlier called fundamentalist liberalism also falls under the heading of humanism and is, therefore, according to this account, incompatible with conservatism.)

The humanist enemy now presents itself in much more subtle and elusive forms, and it is the task of this essay to contribute to the understanding and undermining of those forms. In the context of this task, the main theme of respect has at least three roles. At their most abstract, the call for 'respect' (for people, as opposed to God) signals a deep, false and potentially disastrous humanism. More immediately, it suggests attempts by governments, with little or no interest in anything deep or long term, to paper over cracks in society and to sidestep issues. And, finally, it is likely to be used to stifle exactly the kind of robust free speech that we need in order to rid ourselves of enslaving fallacies, truth martyred on the altar of mere politeness.

I said I was only a bit of an anarchist. The bit in question does not involve anarchist prescriptions for the abolition of the state and private property, but it is anarchist analysis of the nature of government, shared with most utilitarians, including Jeremy Bentham. That is to say, government should be seen as based not on divine or 'natural' right, but on 'force, fear and fraud' (in David Hume's words). It is no more than the persons, interests and institutions that have acquired a certain kind of authority over you. Laws are just the rules they uphold, and the standard by which they should be judged has to do with whether those rules benefit us as much as they might. Thus, I would seek to demystify law, as understood by humanist lawyers, in much the same way as an anarchist would. And I have an initial sympathy with the Catalan anarchist 'government' of 1937. They shot you after three serious offences, but refused to call it punishment or justify it by invoking the concept of justice. It was just getting rid of you. But here, I must insist again, my anarchism is abstract rather than practical: there is a sound utilitarian case for saying that such practices should not be allowed, because our happiness requires security and consistency in the enforcement and adjudication of rules.

Finally, I must insist that, in signing on for five 'isms', I have not simply turned up at some kind of ideological 'Freshman's Fair' and signed up for everything. I may be several things, but I am not (obviously) a humanist, nor a theist, nor a socialist. And my self-attribution of conservatism may seem strange to those whose conservatism is grounded in religious belief or consists of nostalgia for previous ages, which were supposedly more ordered or more respectful of a 'high' culture. Mine is, in fact, a kind of modernism, which regrets that the direction we appeared to be taking in the 18th century – towards a greater honesty, a concern for liberty and a reliance on reason – was so easily abandoned in favour of a sentimental humanism, which reproduces all the worst features of religion. My title is an immediate reaction to a phrase used by the current government of my country in its dealings with crime and 'deprivation': 'the respect agenda'. But my argument is not meant to be a particular attack on that government or even on the thinking of the 'Left'. The polemic is directed at the much broader and more longstanding phenomenon of unclear and ethically unacceptable thinking that has left governments, like so many ineffectual schoolteachers, feebly pleading for 'respect'.

2

SAY WHAT YOU'RE GOING TO SAY ... AND WHY

The immediate stimulus for this piece of writing – the equivalent of Princip's bullet – was an argument about football. The columnist (and blogger) Theodore Dalrymple had suggested that football represented the worst aspects of our society, and that 'decent citizens' should avert their eyes from the 2006 World Cup.[2] Though not a huge enthusiast of global football or of FIFA and its World Cup, I was keen to argue that I was in favour of anything that would annoy 'decent citizens' (considering myself to be a fairly indecent subject of Her Majesty). More importantly, I did also want to defend some aspects of our culture that, in our own times, are represented by football support: the ribaldry, contempt, humour and obscenity that have made up much of the entertainment on an English football ground. I would not seek to defend some of the very violent behaviour that has been facilitated by the conditions of English football, but I would argue that such behaviour is relatively rare and that disapproving of it raises the very important question of whether the state should be trying to create a society in which people do not want to do bad things, or should merely seek to punish those who do them.

There is no entirely satisfactory name for the aspect of our culture I am talking about, but the least misleading is probably 'misrule'. This would include much of what went on in traditional, rural sport; much of what has thrived in youth sub-cultures since at least mediaeval times; many pre-Christian folk traditions; some forms of rioting; and much else – a fuller analysis to come. In short, manifestations of our refusal to live in a fully ordered society, prescribed by the political correctnesses of the day, whether Catholic, Cromwellian or Blairite. And if the argument had not been about football, it could have been about many other things, including Shakespeare. Since pretty well everybody reveres Shakespeare, he is contested, as ideas and values and religious figures are contested. The evidence is left nicely and tantalisingly vague, so that we can argue about who he was in the very literal sense of that question. But even if that were not the case, there would be a more spiritual contest over who Shakespeare was in his heart. Was he the rather noble, scholarly humanist that many people seem to see in him? Or was he the gloriously theatrical, nihilistic figure that I see, who could give expression to any principle, but who seems convinced by none? (And with something of the street yob in his makeup to boot.)

Between whom do such contests occur? Between Fogeys and Libertines, I would suggest. There is no insult implied in my use of the term 'Fogey'. Many of the people I am thinking of – Theodore Dalrymple and A. N. Wilson being prime examples – are proud to use it of themselves. Fogeys are conservative and a little snobbish, insofar as they favour the ways associated with high status rather than low. No dissent so far, from me at least. But they do tend to give a narrow construction to those ways, and they have a suspicious love of social order and harmony. I use the term 'Libertine' precisely because all the other terms that might be applied to those who love freedom and happiness have been mangled and misused to the point that they must be abandoned. 'Liberal' in the USA now means the precise opposite of what it traditionally meant, and there are 'libertarians' for whom liberty is merely a kind of technicality in which the civil law (say) replaces the criminal law as a series of restrictions on conduct. And 'neo-liberal' has been widely used to refer to post-Soviet *étatistes*. So, if you really believe that people should be as autonomous as possible, and preferably have a hell of a good time, then 'Libertine' it is. And if I'm the only one, so be it.

This is not a dispute between religious and unreligious believers *per se*. For example, as a Libertine, I would put both

Matthew Arnold and V. I. Lenin very high on the list of men I most detest. Both regarded most of what 'ordinary' people like as corrupted and, in some sense, 'false'. Both wished to educate everybody to serve some collective good. Both wanted a state run by intellectuals that will seek to elevate us. Neither understood – and both generally opposed and mistrusted – markets. Yet Arnold was an Anglican poet, writer and inspector of schools, while Lenin was a Communist revolutionary (and the son of an inspector of schools, though I will resist the temptation to identify the enemy too specifically). Still less is it a dispute between 'Left' and 'Right' as they are normally conceived. Some American 'conservatives' are so far from my libertine position that they might as well be Communists, and this has also been the case with some English Conservatives in the past. However, the main sources of irritation that have stimulated the creation of this particular polemic in my time and in my place are very much identifiable with the Left, for reasons that will become obvious, if they are not already.

The particular bone of contention here is not football or Shakespeare, but respect. People want to be respected. The government wants us to respect them, each other, 'minorities', the social order. Never was so much respect wanted by so many from so many others. No sooner had Tony Blair begun his third term as prime minister in May 2005, than he said he wanted to put the creation of a 'culture of respect' at the heart of his government's aims.[3] The then leader of the Conservative Party, Michael Howard, disagreed with him only on whether he meant it, commenting: 'We had no idea he was thinking what we were thinking' (a play on one of his own party's election slogans). Of course, he wanted 'delivery' rather than the 'fizzy rhetoric' on offer.[4] The radical group led by George Galloway that broke away from Labour actually uses the word in the party's name: 'Respect – the Unity Coalition'. As I was writing this passage, I switched on the radio. It was *Any Questions*, and a woman was talking of the need to teach people to respect minorities and the environment. I have no idea whether she was a politician and, if so, from which party; for this sort of droning has become just background noise, like bees in a summer garden. As if this were not enough, gangsters and street urchins demand respect. *Uomo di rispetto* is, according to John Dickie, one of the two or three phrases that *Mafiosi* use to define themselves.[5] This has been passed on to every kind of gangster, and even small children bristle if they think you are 'dissing' them (as in being disrespectful).

I will argue that this obsession with respect illustrates the nature of the incoherence of the age. At the time of writing, Islam apart, we are faced with no potential tyrants with the level of conviction about 'What is to Be Done' that was possessed by Lenin or Arnold. Rather, there is a more devolved and decadent form of tyranny, which insists that we try to keep all moralities in being, rather than imposing one of them. While I admit that this contemporary threat is less menacing, I also think it is a good deal more worthy of contempt. Certainly, one should be fearful of those who believe they know the one truth and the one route to salvation, but at least they can be coherent, and *if* they happened to be right... By contrast, there is something pathetic about belief in belief, postmodernism laced with unreflecting enthusiasm. It reminds me of the transition from the Lancashire of my youth to the California of my young adulthood. In the former, if one said something outrageous, people would say 'You're talking bollocks!' (possibly, even, 'Th'art talking bollocks!'). In the latter, they would say 'That may be true for you...', an expression that I take to exemplify multiculturalism at its most absurd.

It also reminds me of the late Sir Peter Ustinov, whose unctuous belief in belief and cosmopolitan background led him to be more or less in favour of everything, and keen to get everybody round a table to discuss the great verities. This was expressed through his involvement in the Issyk-Kul forums, and also came across in an interviewing style that was so respectful that it bordered on the nauseating. But here is an expression of this kind of pan-theological position, from a late play called *The Old Man and Mr Smith*. Mr Smith is talking to God:

There is much condemnation in the various holy writs about praying to false gods, to idols with feet of clay, all that internal propaganda, publicity put out in favour of one belief at the expense of all others. This seems to me entirely erroneous, in that it is belief itself which is important, not the objects of belief. Belief entails a lesson in humility. It is good for man's soul to believe in something greater than himself, not because he magnifies his god, but because he shrinks himself to size. Now, if this is so, a primitive man who worships a tree, or the sun, or a volcano derives the same benefit from his act of moral prostration as a cultivated man would do before the god of his tradition, and the effects on the worshipper are identical. It is the act of worship which is important, at no time the object of that worship... Many heretics have been burned and hideously tortured because they worshipped false gods. They should have been congratulated for worshipping at all.[6]

I start with a prejudice in favour of Sir Peter, who once came to see me act (though it may have been relevant that his daughter Tamara was also in the cast), and I share his distaste for Inquisitions and heresy trials; but otherwise I regard this passage as almost definitive of a kind of contemporary malaise, which I am seeking to attack: worship as therapy? Belief necessary for humility? Try remembering that you are an improbable bio-chemical accident! Or looking up at the stars. But it is the reverence for reverence that is important here and the clue to the mentality of those who call upon us to respect one another's beliefs. If you really assembled everybody to talk about the nature of truth and reality, they would start an irresoluble theological argument culminating in war. Only disbelief can really save us. Encouraging belief only allows the Catholics to continue stunting and misleading the Catholics; the Muslims ditto.

I am going to argue that governments should not be trying to manipulate us into respecting each other. This is partly because I will also be arguing that their understanding of respect is not merely incoherent, but contradictory, and that, in one sense of respect, governments could not possibly achieve this objective. Also that, insofar as they do try to inculcate respect, we should resist. Furthermore, to different degrees we should actively pursue policies of non-respect in our private lives – one such policy being contempt. But we should embrace some of the things that might fall under the heading of respect – these could include tolerance, politeness and affection. In some respects, the structure of my argument will resemble that of Samuel Smiles in *Self Help*. Smiles famously argued that '...the value of legislation in human advancement has been much over-estimated'.[7] But, unlike many 20th-century libertarians, he did not view the state as hugely menacing, but more as an irritating nuisance, prone to fall into the hands of interfering fools. Its worst effect is that people come to expect from it improvements in society, which it cannot deliver and which can only really be achieved by individuals acting on their own behalf. Thus he has a political argument – that states should not attempt tasks they are not suited to – and also an ethical argument – that we should act as if our fate lies in our own hands, and largely ignore public projects that might contribute to our improvement. The ethical argument is a good deal more important than the political. So it will be in what follows: the ethical argument that we should, individually, develop and exercise our various capacities for non-respect is more important than the political argument that states should not have respect policies. The 21st-century state may be more menacing than its 19th-century counterpart, but it is mercifully feeble compared with 20th-century versions.

My case against respect is utilitarian in nature. Many people assume a kind of utilitarianism, but blur it with something quite different – in many respects its opposite. As I have said, this 'something' can be broadly described as 'humanism', which transfers most of the properties of God to an abstracted conception of humanity. The best-known aspect of this is the transfer of our fundamental idea of the source of sovereignty from God to 'the people', but it is equally important that the source of rules should become a calculation of the logical consequences of the nature of the human condition. Thus the philosopher Immanuel Kant was able to come up with as many rules and duties, which followed inexorably from our nature as rational agents, as the Church had based on the will of God. Indeed, modern philosophers have attributed to Kant the most profound sense of 'respect' – namely his doctrine that we should treat other people *as ends in themselves* rather than as means.

Perhaps the most typical political doctrine of humanism is that all people have 'rights', simply because they are people. These rights are 'natural', 'human' and 'inalienable'; they may or may not be extended to other entities, but they cannot be withdrawn from people. Utilitarians have always been definitively opposed to this doctrine, regarding it as the humanist equivalent of the religious conception of natural law, which must be obeyed whatever the consequences (a close relation being the doctrine of Julius Caesar's father-in-law, Calpurnius: *Fiat iustitia, ruat coelum*, usually translated as 'Let justice be done, though the heavens fall'). This opposition is clearest in Jeremy Bentham's attack on natural rights in *Anarchical Fallacies* and in his essay on torture (of which he is bound to approve, under certain circumstances).[8]

Although 'religion' and 'humanism' are normally understood to be opposites, from the point of view of utilitarian ethics they have many similarities. 'Humanity' as an elevated and abstract concept is broadly similar to 'God'. According to a theist claim, man was created in God's image. And, according to a humanist claim, when man looks for an image of God, he can see no further than his own (higher) nature. The nature of God and of humanity both serve as the sources of rules that we are required to obey, and the obedience will sometimes conflict with our calculation of the best aggregate consequences. Humanists, after all, don't actually behave very differently from Christians in 'western' societies. The principal difference that ought to distinguish theistic religion from its humanist descendant is *revelation*: any process by which God's will can be revealed apart from our use of reason –

typically the appointment of a prophet, the dropping of tablets of stone, etc. It is, however, fairly apparent that much supposed religion – including that of Immanuel Kant and much of Anglican theology – is merely formal, in that it rejects, whether in theory or in practice, the possibility of revelation, and makes the same sorts of calculation as does humanism about the rules to be applied in society.

One low-level humanist doctrine often invoked in politics – that society should be 'caring' and 'compassionate' – ought to be subject to particular utilitarian scorn. There could be no worse rule than a rule of generalised empathy, which requires everybody to care about everybody else – if you believe that is possible. Its implication is that, because some people are miserable, everybody should be miserable. About 3,000 people a day die in the United Kingdom, and there is no point in pretending that we care about them dying. Far better, from a utilitarian point of view, to delight in obituaries.

Robert Goodin has argued that the larger in scale a decision is, the more unavoidable it is that we conceive it in purely utilitarian terms.[9] In deciding whether to drop an atomic bomb on Hiroshima, you must weigh the lives of hundreds of thousands of people against the prolongation of global war by years. It is the definitive modern ethical decision, and in making it, the trappings and niceties of humanism fall away. Can you treat people as having rights and still atomise them? Or pretend they are 'ends in themselves'? Can you blow people up respectfully? Even if you think that this decision was made wrongly or that the dilemma is a false one, you can rest assured not only that we could devise hypothetical dilemmas that are real, but also that, in the course of the 21st century, there will be further dilemmas of the kind supposedly exemplified by Hiroshima.

In short, in debating a variety of issues, I will be taking the side of utilitarianism and lack of respect against the tradition of humanism, which wants us to respect people just for being people or (which is slightly different) for being what they are, whatever they are. Immanuel Kant can be seen as the captain of the opposition team, but its 20th-century players must be taken to include John Rawls and Bernard Williams, both of whom were given prominence for finding objection to utilitarianism as demeaning to human dignity or integrity. In the spirit of the sort of examples that Williams set the reader, the utilitarian is always likely to be asked: 'Would you really have an innocent person flogged in public if you thought the deterrent value and the entertainment value outweighed the pain caused?' To which the answer must be: 'Undoubtedly. Definitely. If the circumstances arose. Perhaps enthusiastically.' After all, if you are prepared to justify the dropping of an atomic bomb...

Which makes utilitarianism sound not very nice. So it is important to redress the balance. Utilitarianism, after all, believes that people should be happy, and much (though not all) of what people seek to achieve through doctrines of the intrinsic value of humanity and the need for respect can be prescribed under other headings.

CONSIDERATION

By definition, utilitarianism believes that all people should be considered. People are any beings that are self-conscious (taken to be co-extensive with a capacity for articulate expression) and sentient. Arguably, all sentient beings should be considered to some extent. Being considered means that you are included in the arithmetic, at least of public decisions. It may mean, of course, that you get nothing out of having been considered: 'We've taken your interests fully into consideration and now we're going to shoot you.'

TOLERANCE/TOLERATION

There are two main reasons for tolerating as much as is sustainable in society. The first is the fundamental one that happiness is normally best served by allowing people to pursue their own interests in their own way. The second, which applies principally to beliefs, is that they may be right. Tolerance is entirely compatible with contempt: you may say

'I find the doctrines of your religion incoherent and its practices craven and distasteful, but I have no wish to prevent you from practising it either by private action or by public legislation.' I have lived nearly all my adult life with a Roman Catholic whose religion I insult daily, but, for her part, she seems unconcerned by my view, and I drive her to church when she is in a hurry or when it is raining. Toleration, in its most specific sense, can be taken to refer to the specific change of assumptions in England and the British Empire after 1689, when the private expression of a variety of religious beliefs became permissible. Toleration allowed (and partly created) the existence of second-, third- and nth-class citizens who did not have the rights of male, propertied Anglicans, but who were allowed space to develop in many different ways, and in some cases it was the citizens of lower grades (particularly the Quakers) who thrived most and contributed most. This was part of what I will be describing as the 'Hanoverian Solution', in which we learned valuable lessons that we have partly forgotten, viz. that unorthodox belief is not necessarily a threat to society, and that a head of state must be accepted, but he or she does not have to be liked, revered, respected or regarded as the Lord's anointed.

In many ways, homosexuality provides a case – arguably even a paradigm case – for toleration, and no more than toleration. 'The quantity of pleasure being equal...' (pushpin is as good as poetry) applies exactly, and there have even been suggestions that Bentham had it in mind. But homosexuality cannot produce children, and cannot be an intimate part of the sort of family life that is an important mechanism of social stability. To claim some sort of equal respect for homosexuality, beyond tolerance, seems pointless and potentially unsustainable.

Thus some substantial part of what really benefits people when they get the 'respect' that they want is either tolerance or toleration. Tolerance here refers to the social space left to people to choose their own way of life, whereas toleration has historically referred to the legal space, though the two words are often used interchangeably.

POLITENESS

It is true that impoliteness can be enormous fun and very amusing:

> Sheriff Bart (Cleavon Little): Good morning, ma'am.
> And isn't it a lovely morning?
> Little Old Lady: Up yours, nigger.
> (Mel Brooks, *Blazing Saddles*, 1974)

But, for the most part, impoliteness makes people unhappy, and politeness makes them happy; and this is true if you define politeness relatively narrowly, in terms of the particular conventions operating at a specific time and in a specific place or, more generally, in terms of a spirit of pleasantness and acquiescence. Therefore, one should endeavour to be polite, unless there is a very clear reason for being impolite. Politeness in this sense is not respect. One can be polite to other people, irrespective of whether one respects them in any sense (I am conscious that I have not yet explored the meaning of 'respect'). Moreover, as a rule of thumb, it can generally be assumed that the less people expect to be respected, the more they will appreciate politeness. Which means, prudence apart, that one should always endeavour to make polite conversation to the cleaning lady, and make a point of remarking to the boss, from time to time, that he is a wanker.

CHARM

Charm takes the principle of politeness one step further. It can be defined as successful efforts that go beyond the bounds of convention in making people feel good about themselves. As with politeness, there is no theoretical relationship to respect, and, in practice, there may even be an inverse relationship. Charm can be exercised in any kind of social relationship, but it does not necessarily work on every person – some people are too twisted or warped to understand the simple benefits of charm. Of course, a utilitarian should be in favour of charm: exercising it, developing it and responding positively to it. It is probably most difficult and most important to use charm on familiar people. Familiarity may breed contempt, but there is no need for it to breed charmlessness.

BENIGN INDIFFERENCE

Most unhappiness arises from malice, from the desires people have to hurt each other, interfere with each other, thwart and humiliate each other, and so on. Thus important and traditional questions arise in ethics and political theory about the nature and origins of malice. I am going to assume that malice is entirely psychopathological. That is, it is not 'natural', insofar as it is possible to bring a child up to be entirely unpathological, but psychopathological conditions are fairly normal (and, with the breakdown of family structures, increasingly common). Malice has nothing, in origin, to do with ideas. By which I mean that, if everybody was brought up by two parents who loved their children and one another, most of the evil in the world would not exist; and also that the question of the emotional conditions in which your personality is created is far more important than whether you are a Muslim, a Jew, an existentialist, etc. (This was an interesting theory about politics developed by Harold Lasswell. It remains a kind of intellectual cul-de-sac for extraneous reasons, but it will be further examined in this book.) However, ideas can be the dangerous catalyst for evil, magnifying its scope and allowing the street bully to become the Grand Inquisitor, Führer, Secretary of the Communist Party, etc. Evil does not arise out of indifference, but it may require more than indifference to oppose it.

Which means that, just as William Morris argued that there would be no political activity or discussion in a future Communist society, so I suggest that benign indifference would be the universal condition in a good society. However, in a real society we need to cultivate acerbic scepticism. Thus I am opposed to any attempts to protect belief – especially religious belief – from 'offence' or 'insult'. I have always argued that academic freedom in particular, and intellectual freedom in general, is nothing unless it includes the freedom to offend. In the 1980s, this argument was directed mainly towards deranged forms of feminism, though in the early 21st century you would not formulate it without thinking primarily of Islam and the high propensity of many of its faithful to feel 'insulted'. Purely selfishly, the protection from insult has no appeal for me, since nobody ever seems to want to ban the things that offend me: a random sample including manifestations of republicanism, the European Union flag, sartorial expressions of Islamism and some Southern English accents.

If there were an essential and inalienable right of human beings, it would be a right to free expression (and a corresponding duty to put up with being offended, insulted and disagreed with). Those who have favoured a strong protection of free speech on the grounds that, in the long run, we can only benefit from a vigorous competition in ideas have usually accepted limitations only on the form of expression, rather than its content. John Stuart Mill's classic example is that we must be allowed to say anything we want about the Corn Laws, but not necessarily to a drunken mob in front of a corn merchant's house. Nobody, I imagine, would want to defend a right to shout 'Fuck off' very close to the ears of passing old ladies as an example of free speech. Which has traditionally generated a line-drawing problem about what can be said where. But technological change has eased that problem: the existence of the internet, the plethora of television channels and the low fixed costs of book production all mean that consumers of ideas have to make positive choices when they consume, so that they need little protection. Indeed, I think it is perfectly coherent to be an extremist in both – opposite – directions of Mill's once-difficult distinction. That is, one could be in favour of no restrictions at all on the expression of ideas in books, on websites and in magazines, but also of very stern restrictions on what might be shouted in the street or said to a public assembly.

Courts in a number of European countries and the European Court of Human Rights have shown a disturbing tendency to limit free speech and to protect religious belief from 'insult'. There is also the question of 'Holocaust denial': it may be absurd and offensive to 'deny' the Holocaust, but most things that human beings believe are absurd – and offensive to somebody. Even though there has often been vigorous opposition to such restrictions on free speech, the vigour has often been exercised on the rather feeble grounds of dangerous precedents and the thin ends of wedges: as if we would like to institute such protection, but where would it stop? And how do we define religion? As an alternative, I am here suggesting that the liberal ideal of a competition of ideas cannot be met by a feeble and pusillanimous form of competition, but only by a culture of scorn and scepticism. A liberal, multicultural society must be one in which cultures are allowed to express a cheerful contempt for each other. We should not be tempted by the wrong kind of tolerance, one that merely devolves tyranny from states to 'communities'.

These arguments must now be explored in particular contexts, such as the problem of dealing with an underclass, the dilemmas and inadequacies of modern education, and the difficulties that arise from having to have democratic politics. But before that, I must examine the concept of respect, as well as some aspects of history that might explain how 'respect' came to seem to be so important.

3

THE CONCEPT OF RESPECT

The equivalent of 'Pawn to King Four' in academic life is to say, of any concept, that it is a) complex, and b) contested – and these are fair points to make in respect of 'respect'. In modern English usage, this one word encompasses what, in the languages from which ours is descended, is a range of concepts. I will deal here with the two main roots. In Latin, there is *reverentia* and *observantia*. The former implies admiration, positive appraisal; while the latter means essentially recognition – for example, in the diplomatic sense, where recognising a state and therefore respecting its boundaries has nothing to do with believing it or its rulers to be of any value. In German, the distinction is between *Respekt* and *Achtung*. The first suggests of its object that we approach it with caution; it acknowledges power and danger. *Achtung*, though known to my generation of English schoolboys for meaning 'Attention' (as in *Achtung, Spitfire*), is also the word Kant uses to denote respect for the person, the treating of people 'as ends'. It is (of course) true that these Latin and German pairs do not carry the same distinction; it is also the case (and is only slightly less obvious) that neither of the pairs of words exhausts all aspects of 'respect' as it is discussed in contemporary English.

There is, naturally, an academic debate as to whether we should distinguish three or four or five or more senses of respect (numbering of senses being as essential to academic life as 'naming of parts' is to the military). The context is that respect has become an important concept in moral philosophy, with some claiming it to be at the heart of the American ethical debate. However, one should be very careful about the philosophical numbers game. Isaiah Berlin wrote memorably about 'Two Concepts of Liberty'. He later expanded it to four, but generations of philosophy and politics undergraduates have shown an ability to churn out a mangled and oversimplified, but recognisable, version of the two ('positive' and 'negative'). By contrast, I remember Alasdair McIntyre starting a lecture with something like: 'If I say "I have a right to X" there are seventeen distinct things that I might be taken to mean.' McIntyre was a good lecturer and an original thinker, but I don't suppose anybody present at the lecture remembered more than two of the senses. Seventeen senses, like Professor Higgins' 134 vowel sounds, is just too many.

But, as it happens, I think there are only two important and essentially different meanings of respect. They correspond roughly to the difference between *reverentia* and *observantia*, but since languages have quite different connotations and nuances, I will now make the distinction entirely in English:

SENSE 1: Admiration of, or deference to, personal qualities. An additional complication is that we don't have to respect a person as such, but can limit our respect to a particular quality or qualities (as in: 'I have the utmost respect for his administrative abilities, but I'm afraid he's one of the most boring men I've ever met').

SENSE 2: Acknowledgement or recognition of right. Thus one must 'respect' the referee or the policeman, even while regarding them both as idiots. There are as many senses and types of respect as there are of rights. Thus there are authority rights (to *prima facie* obedience) and property rights (to exclude, transfer, etc.), and we must respect those in authority and those who hold property. There are also diplomatic rights, varying from recognition of the flag of truce to acknowledgement of sovereign borders. These rights might variously be located in bodies of law or in the weaker and (even) more contestable location of social convention: sovereign borders are justified by international law, whereas the flag of truce is an ancient convention, long pre-dating any idea of the international legal system. If I tell a child to respect an old man because he is old, I am referring neither to legal rights, nor to the old man's particular virtues, nor yet to the utilitarian duty to be nice unless there's a good reason not to be, but to a social convention that exists, to varying degrees, in most societies.

One sense I want to exclude from respect is that in which, for example, an experienced walker might tell you that you must respect the moor or the mountain, meaning that you should be aware of its nature and the dangers inherent in that nature. This is roughly equivalent to the German *Respekt*. It would be odd to say in English that one 'respects' the gangs of youths who hang around the town centre, but this makes perfect sense in its German equivalent. Although it does share an origin (and although in some ways it overlaps and in other ways is analogous), I am going to treat this as a separate meaning of the word 'respect', rather than as part of the concept, because it lacks the ethical dimensions implicit in the concept.

Having cleared that ground (to use the metaphor favoured by philosophers since John Locke), there is an important inference to draw, which is that the two main meanings of respect have very different ethical and logical properties. In the sense of the recognition and acknowledgement of rights, anyone who should be respected is entitled to that respect: it belongs not to a person as such, but to an institution. But nobody is entitled to be admired: admiration is a personal and subjective evaluation, arising spontaneously from the values of the admirer. To be respected in this sense is not something you should ever want and, since I admire autonomy, wanting to be respected would pretty much preclude the possibility of being respected. Indeed, the historical character I most respect is the 1st Duke of Wellington, who wouldn't have given a damn whether I respected him or not. This can be generalised as a First Law of respect: if you want it, you shouldn't be given it, in the personal sense. It is also odd that governments should specifically seek to inculcate respect: in the sense of acknowledging rights, then that is saying no more than that laws are laws and crimes are crimes. And in the sense of personal admiration, such cultures already exist in most cases, enforced by people who do not want to be 'dissed'.

It is worth noting that our language is somewhat confused about the absence or inverses of respect. In principle, it should be like money, with three possible conditions: money (positive) ... no money (zero) ... debt (negative). Thus: respect (positive) ... no respect (zero) ... disrespect (negative). But the zero position doesn't really exist: 'lack of respect' is treated as equivalent to disrespect in most cases. In any case, there is an alternative, stronger negation – in the form of contempt. So, in opposing appeals for us to show 'respect' in clustered and undefined ways, I will sometimes be prescribing indifference, sometimes mere disrespect, and sometimes contempt. Sometimes this will be raging contempt, sometimes cheerful contempt; at its best, it will be cheerful, raging contempt.

4

THREE HISTORICAL REFLECTIONS

1. THE HANOVERIAN SOLUTION

Although I have tried to travel as much as I could afford, I have lived in the same town pretty well all my adult life. When I walk out of our house, which is close to the town centre, it is always the case that I know some of the people I see. That man once sold me a car; I knew that woman once rather better than I do now; that couple over there are the parents of my youngest son's second-best friend; decades ago, I once had a fight with that man coming this way, and we have always said 'Hello' ever since. And that fairly young man has bowled me with his in-swinging Yorker more times than I like to think about. All of which comes together to form a sense of belonging, which is much enhanced by the street names. It gives me enormous pleasure that the winner of the symbolic historical struggle for the control of street names, the centre of an apparent cult of personality, is a fat, lascivious playboy, vain enough to think of himself as Adonis. If things had gone very badly, I might have been walking down Hitler Street or Lenin Avenue. Or the streets might have been called after some deeply earnest person from this very county, like one of the Arnolds or George Eliot. But in the real world (so much better than most of the worlds that might have existed), I walk down Regent Street, past the Regent Hotel and Regent Place, ignoring the Regent Arcade, but stopping to marvel at the price of apartments in the new Regent Gardens development.

And reflecting that, for all his eponymous victory, 'Prinny', George IV, 'Beau' Nash's 'fat friend' (according to 'Beau' Brummel), 'the fourth and last of the fools and oppressors called George' (according to Byron), must be one of the most studiously insulted men in history and surely the most dissed monarch. Charles Greville pulled no punches when he wrote:

> A more contemptible, cowardly, selfish, unfeeling dog does not exist than this King...with vices and weaknesses of the lowest and most contemptible order.

While Walter Savage Landor was relatively kind to George IV in the context of the rest of the dynasty:

> I sing the Georges Four
> For Providence could stand no more.
> Some say that far the worst
> Of all was George the First.
> But yet by some 'tis reckoned
> That worser still was George the Second.
> And what mortal ever heard
> Any good of George the Third.
> When George the Fourth from earth descended,
> Thank God the line of Georges ended.

Though, of course, George was succeeded by his brother, William IV, of whom one obituary remarked that no one should regret the passing of such an odious man.

There was, and is, a very serious implication of all this disrespect, which was fully grasped in the first half of the Hanoverian period by the philosopher David Hume, here writing as a historian:

> By deciding many important questions in favour of liberty, and still more, by that great precedent of deposing one king and establishing a new family, it [the Glorious Revolution] gave such an ascendant to popular principles, as has put the nature of the English constitution beyond all controversy. And it may justly be affirmed, without any danger of exaggeration, that we, in this island, have ever since enjoyed, if not the best

system of government, at least the most entire system of liberty, that ever was known amongst mankind.[10]

In more philosophical mode, in his essay 'Of the Protestant Succession', Hume offers a different dimension of this analysis:

> The advantages of the HANOVER [*sic*] succession are of an opposite nature, and arise from the very circumstance, that it violates hereditary right; and places on the throne a prince, to whom birth gave no title to that dignity. It is evident, from the history of this island, that the privileges of the people have, during near two centuries, been continually upon the encrease, by the division of the church-lands, by the alienations of the barons' estates, by the progress of trade, and above all, by the happiness of our situation, which, for a long time, gave us sufficient security, without any standing army or military establishment. On the contrary, public liberty has, in almost every other nation of EUROPE, been, during the same period, extremely upon the decline...[11]

'Opposite' here means to the advantage of having an undisputed hereditary claimant to the throne. In Hume's view, the Hanoverians made excellent monarchs precisely because they lacked both virtue and legitimacy – and thus, in the terms I defined earlier, were unworthy of respect in either major sense. Charles I had been both virtuous and legitimate, and look where that had got him... More importantly, look where it had got the rest of us!

The sixth and final volume of Hume's *History of England*, along with many of his political and even ethical essays, is permeated with a sense of relief that the ideological and religious enthusiasms of the previous century, and the consequent civil wars and show trials, are behind us. In ideological terms, nobody won: Hume is probably (even) more contemptuous of the (Lockean) view that government must be based on a social contract involving the entire people than he is of the Tory notions of divine right and passive obedience; but that is only because the former were more fashionable and powerful in his own times. You should accept government not because it is appointed by God, nor because it is made legitimate by its contract with the people, but because the consequences of having government (and of accepting it) are much better than the alternatives. Thus Hume's rather wry comment on William of Orange, to the effect that, though his virtues weren't much to write home about and it is best to turn a blind eye to his claim to the throne, the *consequences* of his availability and his calm pursuit of his own interests make him one of the greatest benefactors of mankind. This distinction between rights, virtues and consequences is the most important distinction we can make – particularly, perhaps, in the making of foreign policy by powerful states – and we tend to underestimate it. If the Heavens are really going to fall, forget the rather incoherent convention we call 'justice'.

In general, forget doctrines, accept the framework offered by government, and get on with it. 'It', here, is arts, letters, natural philosophy, industry, agriculture, trade, exploration... Under their provincial North German rulers, generally disliked and scorned and variously inarticulate, fat, mad, vain, etc., the British progressed to an almost unimaginable degree, moving, for the first time in 1,300 years, beyond the levels of prosperity and population that had existed in Roman times, laying the foundations of a global commercial empire and an English-speaking world (both of which are doing a good deal better in the 21st century than they were in the 20th), and making unprecedented strides in all branches of knowledge. Fat Prinny may not have been much in himself, but every kind of human achievement – from invention to the creation of financial institutions to poetry and novels and military tactics – thrived as never before or since. In no particular order, the following were active when Prinny was head of state: the Duke of Wellington, Lord Byron, Jeremy Bentham, Sir Stamford Raffles, George Stephenson, Sir Walter Scott, Jane Austen, J. M. W. Turner, Samuel Whitbread, William Wilberforce,

John Keats, Percy Shelley, Mary Shelley, John Constable, William Blake, David Ricardo, William Cobbett, William Wordsworth, Thomas Bewick, Robert Southey, Samuel Taylor Coleridge, James Mill and the Reverend Thomas Malthus. Can our age compete with their achievements? Could any?

Note the nature of the political achievement that Hume described in the 1750s. What we have that is best is not a system of government, but a system of *liberty*. The Hanoverian Solution was based on a monarch that true monarchists could not really believe in, and an official religion that was somewhat uncertain in doctrinal matters and even rather opposed to religious enthusiasm. It *tolerated* almost everything, but disdainfully, and, insofar as it had 'citizens', it had not just first- and second-class citizens, but went down to nth-class. Aristocrats...property-owning Anglicans...and then on down to the poor, the non-conformists, Roman Catholics... But in every case, there was the space made by tolerance and political stability for Quakers to found banking dynasties, for humble artisans to patent inventions, for sailors to seek their fortunes on the high seas, and for radicals to write their poems and pamphlets. All of which space had been closed down in the 17th century by repressive government, religious fanaticism and civil war, both cold and hot.

Hume insists that the prevailing (Whig) view of the successful constitution of Britain is incorrect:

> It is no wonder, that these events have long, by the representations of faction, been extremely clouded and obscured. No man has yet arisen who has payed an entire regard to truth, and has dared to expose her, without covering or disguise, to the eyes of the prejudiced public. Even that party amongst us, which boasts of the highest regard to liberty, has not possessed sufficient liberty of thought in this particular; nor has been able to decide impartially of their own merit, compared with that of their antagonists.[12]

And:

The Whig party, for a course of near seventy years, has, almost without interruption, enjoyed the whole authority of government; and no honours or offices could be obtained but by their countenance and protection. But this event, which, in some particulars, has been advantageous to the state, has proved destructive to the truth of history, and has established many gross falsehoods, which it is unaccountable how any civilized nation could have embraced with regard to its domestic occurrences.[13]

What is lacking, we might say, in Hume's account is a theory of the necessity of political mythology that might have reconciled him partly to the prevalence of the Whig view. But he might have taken some consolation from the observation that really great minds think alike, and that Voltaire, whom he regarded as a 'Great Poet' by any standards,[14] largely concurred with his understanding of British success. In his *Lettres sur les Anglais*, written during the early years of George II's reign, Voltaire marvelled at a country in which the king did not have to be obeyed, nor respected either as a person or as the Lord's anointed, but merely accepted. And where you did not have to share the king's religion to survive, though it might help if you wanted preferment. Indeed, the king did not have one religion, but at least two, being head of the 'broad' Church of England and the Calvinist–Presbyterian Church of Scotland. Possibly a third, if you counted the family's German Lutheranism. Three religions might look a little insincere, but so long as none of them was Roman Catholicism there was no problem. About a third of the *Lettres* is devoted to the wonder of British religious toleration and the extraordinary discovery that a country can have more than one religion without it mattering much:

If only one religion were allowed in England, the government would very probably become arbitrary; if there were but two, the people would cut one another's throats; but as there are such a multitude, they all live happily and at peace.[15]

In the same letter, nominally about Presbyterianism, he remarks on the City of London:

> There the Jew, the Mahometan, and the Christian transact together, as though they all professed the same religion, and give the name of infidel to none but bankrupts.

According to Voltaire's assessment, the English have produced two great geniuses. One is William Shakespeare, a man 'without the slightest shred of good taste or knowledge of form' who, nevertheless, created brilliant and new forms of theatre. The other is Sir Isaac Newton, who changed our entire conception of how the universe works; he did it, so to speak, despite himself, because Newton's theological writings constitute a vast and vain effort to make his methods and theories co-exist with traditional religious beliefs. All in all, the English achievement is to have thrown away the rule book, to have abandoned the necessities of belief and respect that had stood for a thousand years. In the 17th century, the English were 'normal' within Europe: they had the same religious wars and revolutions as the French and the rest. In the 18th century the English, uniquely, had moved on. It is not that they had answered the big questions, such as 'What does God want?', 'Does all authority come from the people?' and 'What determines the right of rebellion?' It is that they had learned to ignore these in favour of unbridled commerce; and the levels of liberty and prosperity that were furnished by learning that lesson were unprecedented.

Hume, as an historian, was keen to stress that the fanatical cruelties of the 17th century were a thing of the past. However, according to the moral perspectives of a later age, Hanoverian England was a cruel society, even if the cruelty was casual and callous rather than fanatical. Its punishments were notoriously savage, and men and women were flogged, hanged and transported to other continents in large numbers, often for relatively trivial offences. That the English could hang you for stealing a sheep was widely remarked in the rest of Western Europe, though the country had always been known for the severity of its punishments: for example, the observation that English punishments (such as hanging for theft) go far beyond what appears to be sanctioned in the Bible is an issue discussed in the opening part of Sir Thomas More's *Utopia*.

It was also an extremely inegalitarian society, more so than France, though it was successful in minimising the very precise and petty resentments that played such a large part in the French Revolution. The enclosure of land reached its historical peak in the second half of the reign of George III. The aristocracy, but also a new commercial rich, thrived, while the landless poor were probably worse off than in most periods. Foreigners marvelled at the wealth of the country, though a rural way of life was in terminal decline. The rich gambled thousands of guineas on horse races, prize fights and cricket matches, while there were pockets of starvation. It was not yet a society that conceived of 'caring' at the level of the whole. Its high intelligences were not 'intellectuals' in the later sense that they were much concerned with issues that we might now call 'social'. The threats to liberty and stability with which they were familiar came from religious and constitutional schism. That 'the poor' could threaten society as a whole was a perception that grew only late and slowly in the Hanoverian period. The 'condition of England' was something that came to fruition in the 1840s, and its fruits included social work, the social conscience, social policy, sociology, *et al*. Jane Austen's most famous character, Lizzy Bennet, who appears in *Pride and Prejudice*, published in 1819, 'cares' for her sisters, her father, her friends, but cares not a fig for 'society' in our sense.

We should be as wary of the Victorian and post-Victorian narratives of history as social progress as Hume suggests we should be of history as a Whig story of triumph over King and Church. Sir Arthur Bryant sees England as declining from 1815 onwards, as the sense of personal responsibility for one's life, and the very direct and vivid loyalties to village, place and family, began to diminish in an increasingly industrial society.[16]

Even that great maker of Victorian imagery, Tom Hughes, a Christian Socialist, saw great merit in the robust and honest ways of the old England, as represented by Tom Brown's father, a Tory squire. But the general significance of Britain under the Hanoverians is that its rude and robust attitudes, its vigorous freedom from both the concerns of theology and those of humanism ('anthropophilology'?) make it the golden age of disrespect. However reactionary one's tastes, we cannot revive the spirit of another age even if we wanted to. But we should be aware of its achievements and the conditions which allowed them, and be prepared to learn from them.

2. ON RESPECTABILITY

Although Chaucer uses the word 'respect', and although 'respectable', like thousands of other words, dates from Shakespeare's time, 'respectability' came into use only in the 1780s. One of the earliest recorded uses of the word is in a claim that it is possible to be respectable in any social class. It is also acknowledged that the word had derogatory and ironic uses almost from its beginnings. Thus there are hints of ambiguity and contradiction at the core of the idea of respectability. Meaning 1a in the full Oxford English Dictionary is: 'The state, quality or condition of being respectable in point of character or social standing.' But when we talk of 'social standing', we normally refer to a set of established linguistic conventions. There may – there ought to be – a good deal of debate and scepticism about what constitutes the 'middle class', but that does not stop us from talking about it with the same sort of assumption of agreed meaning that we might use for (say) 'bad weather'. This would not be the case with 'character', where we would surely acknowledge that assessment depended on your point of view?

The primary ambiguity of respectability is thus between normative and ethical meanings. It is the same with 'desirability', and John Stuart Mill, no less, commits a messy misunderstanding of this in his *Utilitarianism*. A beautiful and promiscuous woman might be said, without contradiction, to be desirable and undesirable, both in high degree. A four-wheel drive car might equally be respectable and unrespectable: a 'badge of respect' for the driver or owner from their own point of view and that of similar persons, but (arguably) not worthy of our respect – in fact, well worthy of our disrespect. A further complication is that other words with the same apparent logical shape do not work in the same way because there is no ethical version. If I say my car is reliable, I must mean that it *is*, statistically, reliable – not that it ought to be or ought to be regarded as being.

These are dry, conceptual observations, perhaps useful in avoiding confusion or cross-purposes in argument, but not very interesting. They become more lively when we consider the normal and actual consequences of respectability in society, as they were very well remarked by Samuel Smiles:

> Middle-class people are apt to live up to their incomes if not beyond them; affecting a degree of 'style' which is most unhealthy in its effects upon society at large. There is an ambition to bring up boys as gentlemen, or rather 'genteel' men... There is a dreadful ambition abroad for being 'genteel'. We keep up appearances, too often at the expense of honesty; and, though we may not be rich, yet we must seem to be so. We must be 'respectable', though only in the meanest sense – in mere outward show. We have not the courage to go patiently onward in the condition of life in which it has pleased God to call us...[17]

Thus, even if we like the idea of a respectable society in principle, we have to acknowledge that what we are likely to get is a corruption of that principle, a version of mean-responsibility. Smiles is a utilitarian and a libertarian (though not as fanatically anti-state as more recent libertarians – he merely counsels that you can never really expect much from states, rather than insisting on the harm they can do); he wants people to be autonomous and happy. In order to be happy and autonomous, they should avoid debt and dependency of all kinds. A world full of salesmen with unaffordable mortgages, driving large cars they have not paid for, obliged to commute miles to make a living, and feeling obliged to take skiing trips and go on intercontinental holidays in order to avoid losing respect, is as far from a Smilesian good life as it is possible to get, and suggests at least one version of Victorian values from which we could benefit.

This is an important point for both utilitarians and libertarians, because it means that a great deal of what we regard as economic 'growth' or 'progress' fails to make us happier and serves to restrict our freedom. The point has been made many times in parallel forms: Thorstein Veblen's *The Theory of the Leisure Class*, with its account of 'conspicuous consumption' and its distinction between 'ceremonial' and 'instrumental' goods;[18] Vance Packard's *The Status Seekers* in 1959;[19] most rigorously, perhaps, Fred Hirsch's *Social Limits to Growth* in 1976, where the distinction is between 'material' and 'positional' goods.[20] We have been told, consistently, carefully and intelligently, about the dangers of a 'rat race', in which the element of society that is a status competition becomes too dominant; but few of us have taken much notice.

In no age did the importance of respectability become so great as in the reign of Queen Victoria. F. M. L. Thompson calls his history of English social life during the period *The Rise of Respectable Society, A Social History of Victorian Britain, 1830–1900*.[21] Victoria did not become queen, of course, until 1837, but many historians would join Thompson in seeing the forces of Victorianism as gaining strength steadily after the end of the Napoleonic wars in 1815. The mythical and artistic alternative is to be found in Virginia Woolf's *Orlando*, where London turns from colour to shades of grey on the death of William IV. Being an historian, Michael Thompson is little interested in the conceptual analysis of respectability, but he does emphasise an interesting debate about the rise and size of the respectable working class. By implication here, respectability is the most important social phenomenon of the period. It consists primarily in the incorporation (we might now say 'inclusion') of some elements of the working class into the mental condition of the middle class: they want to be educated, to be seen at church, to have money saved, to dress neatly. It is a process that took place, to an even more spectacular degree, in the rest of the English-speaking world, and most of all, perhaps, in Australia, where, two generations into the nation's history, the respectability of the former penal colonies rivalled that of the non-penal colonies, which tended to define themselves in terms of respectability.

There is much to be said for respectability in this context. Insofar as people became more settled, more future-oriented, more prudent and more self-reliant, they might also have become happier and freer. If we are to believe anything of the cheerfully apocalyptic views expressed in the *Communist Manifesto*, respectability was in some kind of competition with revolution: a competition that (in the British Isles at least) it won fairly easily, for which we should be grateful. But there is also very good reason to be suspicious of respectability from my ethical point of view. Smiles' assertion was that it has an enormous propensity to decay into a kind of pseudo-respectability, in which materialism and hypocrisy are major components. And, even more fundamentally, it establishes structures in which petty tyrannies and repressions flourish. Who gets to decide the standards that define respectability? And who gets to interpret them locally? Respectability meant the tyranny of fathers over daughters and of bourgeois magistrates over a hedonistic lower class. The recreations of ordinary people were progressively and deliberately eradicated, especially in the period 1832–63 (from the 'great' Reform Act to the formation of the Football Association). The game of football in Derby (whose legacy is a word in most major languages – such as *il derbissimo* between A.C. Milan and Internazionale Milano) was actually abolished in the 1840s. The number of public holidays, 44 in 1750, had been reduced to four a century later. The felicific calculus of 'social improvement' does not obviously balance out in favour of progress.

This period of recreational repression is well documented; its sexual equivalent less so. Were the Victorians merely coy? Or were they badly frustrated and unfulfilled? We find no equivalents, even in diaries, of the 1st Duchess of Marlborough's gleeful recording of her achievement of two orgasms before her husband had even removed his boots. I think the evidence suggests that the level of repression of women in Victorian society (as in Islam) transcends sexuality. It is the repression of the entire physical side of a woman's being, the awful fiction imposed upon women that they are 'higher', 'more spiritual' beings, reserved for 'refinement', 'accomplishment' and, of course, the one physical strain that cannot be taken from them: reproduction. How different they became from the long-striding, hard-riding, cricketing women of Georgian England! How inevitable that so many bourgeois Victorian women seemed to spend their time nursing psychosomatic disorders on the chaise longue.

Artists and aristocrats kept alive the resistance to bourgeois respectability. As I remarked earlier, there are some important reservations to Victorianism, even in the writing of Thomas Hughes, and the works of Charles Dickens and Anthony Trollope are laced with the sort of meanings that are acknowledged in the Oxford English Dictionary as giving respectability a bad name. Since the early 1960s, respectability has been fairly steadily in retreat. I think this is bound to divide conservatives fundamentally. While I cannot greet it with the sort of one-sided enthusiasm that has been typical of the kind of North London mentality expressed, for example, in Michael Holroyd's simplistic and triumphalist 'Introduction' to Lytton Strachey's *Eminent Victorians*[22] (not least because I think people are nearly always going to be happier if they are brought up by their two biological parents living in the same house), I am prepared to make the utilitarian judgement that the (developed) world is now a happier place, especially because women, who are slightly more than half the total population, can play more sports and entertain more lovers.

3. THE LORDS OF MISRULE

It is 1966 and I am 19 years old, on the London Tube heading for Fulham Broadway and thence to Stamford Bridge, home of Chelsea Football Club. I have half-noticed that the fans on the train are different from what I am used to: they are all male (that is, not even a smattering of women) and all young (rather than being of a normal spread of ages). They all wear jeans and they are louder and more excited than traditional crowds. As one, they begin to sing, to the tune of 'London Bridge is Falling Down':

> 'Arry Roberts is our friend, is our friend, is our friend,
> 'Arry Roberts is our friend: 'e kills coppers.[23]

I am familiar with the new practice of community singing among football fans, but this is very different from the plaintive and sentimental version of 'You'll Never Walk Alone' that I first heard Liverpool fans sing in 1964. I am appalled. Harry Roberts is probably the most notorious criminal in England, having been the ringleader in an incident in which three young policemen were killed. I am from a small town in Lancashire, and I have never heard sentiments like this expressed before. This is not just middle-class innocence; I have been watching football for more than a dozen years without seeing more than the odd bout of fisticuffs or hearing much worse than a vigorous questioning of the quality of the referee's eyesight. Because of my curiously accelerated education,[24] I have spent more than a year of my life as a labourer, and can assure any sociologist who believes otherwise that the 'working-class' people I know hate criminals, not the police. What this incident does is to confirm certain prejudices about London and Londoners that are fairly well entrenched where I come from. What perhaps I might have thought, had I known more about culture, myth and history, is that *the Lords of Misrule* are back.

In its strict sense, a 'Lord of Misrule' refers to the leader of the Christmas revelries in mediaeval England. The appointment had parallels in many other European countries (Abbot of Unreason in Scotland; *Prince des Sots* in France). The revelries were probably akin to the Roman *Saturnalia*, but undoubtedly winter festivities were held by the Saxons, Vikings, etc. In some instances, 'Misrule' was officially sanctioned – for example, by the City of London. It was made illegal in England in 1555, having been in contest with Christian Churches for well over a thousand years, but there are almost certainly many vestiges in our winter traditions, including kissing under the mistletoe and heavy drinking to see in the New Year. It had, in any case, been partly subsumed under, and partly replaced by, the more officially sanctioned and more moderate institution of the Revels, which had an official 'Master of the Revels' – a parallel to the Lord of Misrule.

But what is important to my argument is not these fairly obscure aspects of folklore, but a broader sense of misrule, consisting of all the times and places in which the normal rules – including the requirements of respect – are suspended. As it happens, I had known of one version of such a tradition long before I came across 'football hooliganism'. This was 'Mischief Night' (4 November), during which it was more or less a cultural requirement to do things like knock on doors and run away or throw flour at unsuspecting adults. I was introduced to it by contemporaries, my parents not being from the area. It would appear that this tradition was confined to the Pennines and Scotland, and that it celebrated the setting of the barrels for the Gunpowder Plot of 1605; the following night, of course, we celebrated the demise of the plotters. It is said to have been widely believed that we children had a *right* to our mischief, and that the police were not supposed to act on Mischief Night. Frankly, I never found the whole thing to be much fun, and it is interesting to note that it now seems to have been 'globalised', subsumed under a tradition of Halloween, very much in its American version of 'trick or treat'. This, of course, takes place four days earlier and, for the record, I should say that anything we did to celebrate Halloween was entirely confined to playing games with apples, which tended to be in surplus at that time of year.

One example of an adult version of Mischief Night used to occur as part of the annual hop-picking season in Kent. Up to 4,000 pickers assembled at the largest farm, Beltring, and it was part of the folk tradition that 'hop weddings' were arranged, in which a hop pole was passed over a couple and they lived as man and wife for the picking season. It was, essentially, wife-swapping or 'swinging' before the practice evolved (as it is widely claimed to have done) in the US military in the 1940s. It attracted the interest of Christian organisations, particularly the Salvation Army, thus continuing the centuries-old contest between misrule and Christianity. Mass picking was only replaced by mechanisation at Beltring in 1968: the farm is now a tourist attraction, which advertises its suitability for weddings.[25]

In some cases, the sphere of misrule was defined by place. In particular, forests in European tradition variously represent danger, anarchy, freedom and a different set of rules. This is particularly obvious in folk stories (including the Robin Hood legend and the collections of the Brothers Grimm), but there are interesting versions of this in Shakespeare. Duke Senior, in *As You Like It,* asks rhetorically of the Forest of Arden:

Are not these woods
More free from peril than the envious court?[26]

But it is in *A Midsummer Night's Dream* that the forest most clearly symbolises freedom and fantasy. Virtually everything that is forbidden in the city happens in the forest. Indeed, in most modern productions, where the same actors play Oberon and Titania as play Duke Theseus and Queen Hippolyta, the implication is that Bottom, the weaver, has made love to Hippolyta, thus transgressing almost all the prohibitions that would normally be in force in the city. University campuses have often staged their own versions of midsummer night's dreams, in the form of June leaving parties.

There have been many other spheres of misrule. The whole history of comedy (where not sanitised by censors like the Reithian BBC) is of the creation of stages on which you can say or do things – and show forms of disrespect – that you cannot otherwise do. There was an important element of misrule in the treatment of politicians until relatively recently: the Duke of Wellington, as a prime minister who was also a national hero, had mud thrown at him regularly and had his windows broken. But the form of expression I find most interesting is the link between sport and misrule. Pre-modern sport was almost always associated with riotousness: windows were broken, fences destroyed, enclosed land reoccupied – and this was as true of the urban apprentices as of the rural poor. What seems particularly interesting and complex is that, when sport modernised, it did so in the public schools and with a new set of moral, even religious, meanings: in Tom Hughes' phrase, it was about 'manly piety'. Yet it continued to be a venue for misrule: Matthew Arnold, the son of the very man associated (by outsiders, at least) with the invention of modern and decent sport, referred casually and bitterly in 1868 to 'the crowd at Epsom on Derby day and all the vice and hideousness which was to be seen in that crowd'.[27] Early working-class games of football, in the late 1870s and early 1880s, especially in Lancashire, appear to have been more riotous than at any time in the 20th century. W. G. Grace, the great hero of that age, remained a kind of licensed Lord of Misrule, a sledging, rule-bending, win-at-all-costs superstar – the great Victorian who defied Victorian values and harked back to a bucolic Hanoverian age, as Bernard Darwin and C. L. R. James have argued.[28]

The history of crowd behaviour at Association football matches contains a mystery: between approximately 1926 and 1960 (and longer in most places), football crowds seem to have been very orderly. So, when 'hooliganism' (as it is internationally and near-universally known in its more recent manifestation – the word is used in more than a hundred languages) reappeared, was it a new phenomenon arising out of new conditions, as the majority of researchers seem to have assumed? Or was it the old phenomenon mysteriously revived, having lain dormant as some sort of 'cultural tradition' or 'racial memory', as the Victorians liked to put it ? I don't think this question can be fully resolved, but I do favour the traditional analysis. I first went to football in (I think) 1953, when it was still very orderly; but there was something about the language used and the way in which schoolmasters shouted at referees and tolerated individual fights which suggested, even then, that this was a special zone, where normal morals did not apply. In general, I think culture has great longevity: to take an extreme example, I was taught the superstitious ditty about magpies ('One for sorrow, Two for joy...') by my grandmother, who was born in 1887; she had been taught it by her grandmother, who was born in 1820.

What is both interesting and disturbing about forms of misrule is the ease with which, having been taught 'the difference between right and wrong', we are able to suspend it when the meta-rule is introduced, which says that the rules do not apply at time T or place P. I say 'we' because, apart from Mischief Night, my own chief experience of this was as a player of rugby union. All remained properly within the Arnoldian conception of organised games at school; but, as soon as I entered the worlds of university and adult rugby, there was universal participation in practices which either Thomas or Matthew Arnold would have found hideous and depraved: 'The Engineer's Song', possibly the most obscene thing in the English language, and 'Zulu Warrior', in which men take it in turns to strip naked and be doused with beer, to the accompaniment of a faux-African chant. And the vandalism, the running down the roofs of lines of cars and the removal of street signs... In the 1970s, I was in charge of a student house with a fair number of rugby players and, come the end of the year, I had to remove large numbers of bollards, road signs, traffic lights and so on.

It is worrying to observe how easily people accept the idea of normal rules and decencies not applying in the particular case. It suggests an easy shift towards participation in ethnic cleansing or concentration camps. I once took an American colleague, a liberal and a Jew and the author of a very well-known book on race in America, to his first English football match. As a warm-up, all 4,000 or so of us in the paddock raised an arm, pointed a forefinger at the away supporters and weighed lustily into 'You're going to get your fucking heads kicked in.' My friend was visibly both amused and shocked as he whispered to me: 'I never knew that a Nuremberg rally could be so much fun.' But I would defend the institutions of misrule against the fogeys who seek to condemn them, and against the Lefties who seek to explain them and who imagine they can remove their 'causes'. Mostly, it is naughtiness: they threw mud, not stones, at the Duke, and only a fraction of 1 per cent of those who chant about kicking heads in would ever do so. Admittedly, naughtiness can act as a screen for evil, and often did so at the height of the hooligan period. But it is fun; it has more value than just the functional 'letting off steam'; it offers excitement and self-knowledge as deeper pleasures, which would not be available in a more ordered society. In the Land of Misrule, we share the exhilaration of knowing that nothing should be respected, even though we must acknowledge that, in the morning, some things will have to be accepted.

PART TWO

APPLIED DISRESPECT

5

DO NOT HONOUR THY FATHER AND THY MOTHER

'Honour thy father and thy mother' appears variously as either the fourth or the fifth of the Ten Commandments (though it does not feature at all on the 'second Tablets of Stone' in the Book of Exodus). The Hebrew word in question is transliterated as *kah-bed*, and it has its roots in the idea of weight. In other parts of the King James translation of the Bible, we are exhorted to 'fear' parents, which is the usual translation of *yirah*, which variously refers to awe, reverence, devotion and (of course) respect. The Authorised Version is a good deal stronger on eloquence than on scholarship.

But as a 'commandment', to be treated as a 'rule', it all seems illogical and unacceptable. If the respect (awe, etc.) is of a personal nature, it must be a spontaneous evaluation, and can no more be prescribed than can taste in matters sexual. Actually, out of natural sentiment with an admixture of ignorance, children are likely to honour their parents – be they layabouts or *Mafiosi* – far more than they ought to.

And respect as a right, for anyone who occupies the role of parent, is in crude defiance of all ethical logic. Consider the idea of obligation: this means 'binding oneself', which is not only the original meaning, but also the only clear meaning. You cannot incur an obligation involuntarily; it cannot simply be foisted upon you. The typical way of forming an obligation is to make a promise – a basic ethical concept that extends to a huge category of quasi-promises, including contracts and debts. The most common category of ethical problem occurs in 'relationships', where much promising and quasi-promising is covert and goes unstated. In order to maximise personal responsibility, minimise resentment and ultimately increase happiness, we should, as a guiding principle, try to lower our sense of what other people owe us as far as we can, and be as explicit as we possibly can be about our obligations and those we believe others owe to us.

There is another way of incurring a bundle of obligations, and that is to create someone. This is an issue explored in an interesting way in Mary Shelley's *Frankenstein*, but most of us experience it through natural reproduction. You have many specific obligations to your children and a generalised duty to care for them. There is no inverse of this: they do not choose to be born, they do not choose you as parents and they owe you nothing. Any agreement made by a child, any claimed obligation owed by a child to its parents, must be invalid, given the age dimension and the element of duress caused by the transcendent power of parents over children. In Samuel Butler's *Erewhon*, the Erewhonians do not believe in life after death, but they do believe in life before death. They also believe that birth involves choice (and, therefore, that choosing life is also choosing death), but even they did not believe that you choose your parents.[29]

Of course, it must be stressed that obligation, in the sense defined, can never be a conclusive ethical consideration. I may promise my wife very clearly that I will meet her at 6pm, but then, on my way to the rendezvous, meet somebody in serious distress whom I am able to help: the important non-obligation must take precedence over the trivial obligation. This is very much the satirical point of W. S. Gilbert's libretto for *The Pirates of Penzance*, subtitled *A Slave of Duty*. Frederick has made promises to the criminal pirates and feels obliged to commit crimes. It all hinges on the ambiguity between his having been on the planet for 21 years, and when somebody born on 29 February in a leap year can justifiably be said to have had a 21st birthday. Gilbert's target is clearly Kant, who thinks that morality can be based on precise calculations of duty rather than on broad and decent calculations of consequences. However, the word 'duty' is problematic in this context, because it sometimes seems to refer to obligations and sometimes not. We talk of duty in many different ways, including statutory duties prescribed by governments, where there may be no element of chosen commitment. It is not clear that Frederick has incurred an obligation fairly.

The broad utilitarian case against honouring is that it is a bad rule and we would be better off without it. This is not a trivial matter: this commandment serves to restrict social mobility and it helps keep underdeveloped countries underdeveloped. Enormous misery is caused by people trying to live up to their parents' standards; by people finding themselves hidebound by their parents' limitations; and by people taking too seriously their 'relationship' with their parents. I have been particularly depressed by the misery caused by the pressures of parental expectation, particularly among 'ethnic minorities', in my four decades as a 'personal tutor' (rising, even, to 'Senior Tutor'). If there really is a role for the state in liberating people from the power of other institutions, as 'New Liberals' have been insisting since the 19th century, then it lies in mitigating the effects of family life.

> They fuck you up, your mum and dad.
> They may not mean to, but they do.
> They fill you with the faults they had
> And add some extra just for you.
>
> But they were fucked up in their turn
> By fools in old-style hats and coats,
> Who half the time were soppy-stern
> And half at one another's throats.
>
> Man hands on misery to man,
> It deepens like a coastal shelf.
> Get out as early as you can
> And don't have any kids yourself.

As with the Authorised Version, eloquence triumphs over caution; but Philip Larkin does have a point. I speak neither personally, nor with bitterness. Between the extended family, in which I spent my early years, and the holiday camp with edge (otherwise known as boarding school) where I went when I was ten, I didn't have to worry about my parents too much.

Finally, I must add what any utilitarian must add: that one should be kind to one's parents – tell them jokes, make them cups of tea and reminisce about how nice it was being a child. But you should do this because the world is a better place if you do it, not because you have a duty to 'honour' anybody.

6

A DISRESPECTFUL EDUCATION

Francis Gilbert, author of *I'm a Teacher, Get Me Out of Here* and *Yob Nation,* is not really my cup of tea, and his preferred world of gentleness and sensitivity is not mine. I agree with him, though, that we can trace an image of yobbishness in England back to the nation's beginnings and forward through Shakespeare and the John Bull stereotype. Scratch an Englishman and you find a yob, as Bernard Shaw nearly said. I think Gilbert is in danger of committing the Gramscian fallacy, in which you explain something so completely and systematically that you are also explaining why it cannot be changed. Thus the development of *Marxism Today* up to its demise in 1992 and Gilbert's account of yobs: excessive explanation leads to moral inertia. However, there is a passage at the end of *Yob Nation* that appeals to me:

> I got off the bus clenching my fists. Yes, we need to be aggressively liberal with our children and their parents: we have to force civility and decency down their throats!
> I felt I had gone full circle. My own experiences in the classroom had been at the root of my desire to investigate our yob nation, and from there I had gone on to travel widely round the country to see what was really happening on our estates, in our suburbs, our offices and the corridors of power. Now I was back in the classroom: education could be at the heart of solving our problems. Not wishy-washy, take-it-or-leave-it education, but tough, demanding, insistent education that grabbed people by the throats and ordered them to

listen. Yes, if the decent people learned a few tricks or two [*sic*] from the yobs it could be done.[30]

Of course, I am not offering a complete endorsement of this passage. The word 'liberal' could mean anything here, and the Arnoldian project of teaching 'civility and decency' is also elusive (worse, it smells of a genuinely repressive project of social engineering). But 'tough, demanding, insistent education that grabbed people by the throats and made them listen' could improve the world enormously. As a utilitarian, I regard the world as a potential source of enormous pleasure, most of it unrealised. Here, more than anywhere else – in educational theory – utilitarianism and liberalism part company. The liberal economists' theory of taste, which says that people's tastes are a kind of given (and must be innate in some sense), seems nonsense in this context. Mere negative liberty – letting people do what they want – is just a recipe for unhappiness in children. They have to be 'taken by the throat' and force-fed. But what? The love of life is what I would force down their throats. And the only authentic love of life is the love of detail. How can you *not* be interested in the organisation of the Roman army, the exact value of *pi*, the rock strata visible on the hills above the school, the GDP per capita of Albania, the distribution of the hooded crow...? Even when things are boring, it's interesting to analyse why they are so.

Unfortunately, the evidence suggests that an overwhelming majority of people do not see how interesting the world is or how much fun knowledge can be. They lead miserable, instrumental, nose-on-the-floor lives, wondering how to get a better car or make the payments on the one they already have. The question is *why*? The assumed answer must be that some of them are incapable of doing any better, but that some are. If you could find out how many fell into each category, you would do so. And if you could coerce the improvable into improvement, by whatever means, then surely you would do that? The extent to which contemporary education seems to be desiccated, bureaucratised, instrumentalised and, simply, hopeless at doing the important things it might be doing is enough to make a genteel chap like Francis Gilbert want to take people by the throat. Imagine what a yob like me might want to do to save people from the absence of true pleasure, which is the necessary consequence of ignorance!

——◦◦◦◦——

Scene 1: H. H. Smythe (names changed to protect the guilty) is displeased with the presentation of your 'prep'. It is, he storms, even more unpleasant to look at than its perpetrator. His instinct, he says, is to think of you as a worm, but that would be a foolish error because worms are useful creatures, worthy of preservation. No, you are a slug, an extremely unpleasant and utterly useless creature which consumes food that should go down more deserving gullets...

You listen contentedly to this series of insults, hoping he will come up with something more original, which you can boast about. Being insulted by H. H. is part of what makes you a member of this venerable institution. (Imagine if he never insulted you...) In any case, being 13, and therefore immensely sophisticated in a kind of sub-Freudian way, you believe it is necessary for H. H. to let off steam to compensate for his not having got his end away. He is a bachelor of uncertain age who has been seen, you are reliably informed, dining with a good-looking, but possibly straight-laced, woman in the new Italian restaurant in the town centre. And the longer it goes on, the more satisfied he will be and the less likely to beat you. Most likely he will throw the exercise book at you and tell you to get out of his sight. It's the quiet ones you have to worry about.

——◦◦◦◦——

Scene 2 (a generation later): You have been a bit of a nuisance, telling that other lad what a twat he was, and your work was late and pretty badly presented. And your muttering of 'petty-minded wanker' when Mr Kelly pointed this out was undoubtedly too penetrating. So here you are, closeted in a room with Harry Smythe (he visibly likes you to call him Harry), whose job it is to counsel you. And he tells you how much potential you have, and how highly the school rates your abilities and how sympathetically they understand your frustrations, but...strictly in the interests of achieving the targets you are setting yourself (well ought to be, anyway) we need to think about our behaviour...and – in the real world – presentation matters. So you sit there, not taking any interest because there's nothing he can do. They can, in the end, suspend you, but you're way off that and they'd have to start suspending the really disruptive ones, and they're not going to do that because of the paperwork and the publicity.

—⁓—

Scene 3 (roughly the same time): An Li Chong has requested to see me, insisting that I call her by her preferred name of Daphne. She is a very serious young woman, and somebody in the People's Republic of China is paying good money for her to study International Political Economy for a one-year Master's degree. I have a 'pastoral' responsibility for her: it is to me she must come if she has any problems. She has some questions about the reading list:

> *Daphne*: Here is the list for this week. Is it necessary to read all the books and articles on the list?
> *(It is about three-quarters of a page long.)*
> *Self*: Not literally, no. You do what you can. *(i.e. you skim, you skip, you see how long it takes to decide that it's repetitive or rubbish or repetitive rubbish, and you look at the headings and the tables and the pictures if there are any).*
> *Daphne*: I calculate that it would take 360 hours for me to read all of this. And there are three modules.
> *Self*: Well obviously you can't read it all! Deciding what you can do in the time available is one of the skills you must learn. *(Buzz word, 'skills'.)*
> *Daphne*: Are the authors on this list the most distinguished in the field?
> *Self*: *(How the frick would I know?)* Yes, by and large – we would set the most challenging and important authors.

Daphne: And how long have the professors who wrote these books been studying this subject? *(Strange question! But I think I can see where this is going.)*
Self: Oh, I don't know. Let's say an average of 15 years?
Daphne: So, I come, a poor girl from China, I have to read the writings of many famous professors who have been studying for 15 years and I must read them slowly, in English in one week, and then *(her lower lip wobbles, she is angry and upset)* I have to CRITICISE them!
(You have to admit, from a Confucian perspective. she has a point!)

⎯⎯∿∿⎯⎯

Scene 4 (considerably earlier): Notwithstanding the Oxford tutorial system, Dr X chooses to meet us all together, 12 of us. We have been at university for ten days now, and I, for one, have found the whole thing far too interesting to attempt any academic work. I couldn't get hold of the books anyway. This is the first time we have met; last week was only an introductory organisational meeting. Actually, there are only 11 of us here: Boy Wonder is missing. Dr X is deciding whether to start without him. 'Anyone know where Mr Wonder has got to?' At this point he enters, hyperactive and bony, under a mass of dark curls. 'Ah, Mr Wonder, nice to see you – do sit down.' Boy remains standing; he is carrying at least six books. 'Is this economics?' he demands. 'Well,' says Dr X patiently, 'all of those books are about a particular form of economics called welfare economics, but it is regarded by many people as the basis of the discipline.' Boy drops the books on the floor, where they lie, disrespected. 'It's based on a mistake,' he says, with an I-thought-as-much look on his face. 'And would you like to tell us the nature of this mistake?', asks Dr X. And we all lean forwards. We really, really want to know the answer.

Even Dr Watson would have no difficulty in making the inference that my own education was the model for Scene 1, whereas Scene 2 is about the education of my children's generation. It all seems very sad and Soviet, closely parallel to the old Communist joke: we pretend to learn and they pretend to teach us. They made the best thing in the world boring, bureaucratic and instrumental. In at least the last decade of my (university) teaching career, my principal emotion was pity for the younger generation. They had been fed precise little bits of knowledge and then tested on their capacity to regurgitate them. They had been assessed in some significant way in every year of their lives from the age of seven to 21. (This was true of only four of the years of my education.) No wonder they regarded the whole thing as stressful and yearned to wander off on 'gap years'. They had precious few skills, very little general knowledge, and any originality they might have had was cowed by the need to produce conformist answers. And this was supposed to be the cream of the crop! How on earth had it come to this?

The political answer has to do with democracy and the 'neo-liberal' agenda of accountability. I am not being partisan: the 'Right' is at least as much to blame as the 'Left'. And this is not part of a package of *O Tempora, O Mores* complaints. Many things have got better since I was young, but education is not one of them. The ideological dimension of understanding this disaster is mostly about ideas that have got out of control. I will concentrate on three.

1. EDUCATION FOR ALL: Everybody should have a chance to be educated. Ideally, everybody should acquire some basic skills that will make life easier and make the individual more productive. Not everybody can be a theoretical physicist. Between these two extremes we must decide the overall amount and distribution of education. Fred Hirsch, in *Social Limits to Growth*, written in the 1970s, developed his theory of 'positional goods' to show how it is that, in a capitalist and democratic society (especially a 'post-industrial' one), people will demand escalating amounts of educational qualifications, and how governments will collude in their demands.[31] Hence the higher education expansion, grade inflation, plagiarism, illiterate graduates and the whole contemporary world we are now familiar with. The worst thing is that it creates a culture of deceit, in which people constantly have to pretend to have abilities that they do not have: the most common of these are a broad general knowledge and the ability to write an interesting and original essay. At the time Hirsch was writing, none of this had yet happened to any great extent in Britain, though it had in the USA.

Vilfredo Pareto's pyramid suggests that any capacity is distributed in such a way that, as you move from a higher to a lower level of ability, so the percentage of people who have that capacity goes up. There are very few geniuses, slightly more top-class performers, even more who are pretty good, and so on down to a broad base of the pyramid, which includes the great mass of people who have only very basic abilities. The main modification that has been thought necessary is to give the pyramid a 'bulge', to acknowledge that below the stratum of the ordinary is a smaller stratum of the sub-normal. Most of us accept the truth contained in the idea of the pyramid when we consider the distribution of abilities (and our own place in that distribution) in respect of singing, dancing, football or whatever. But not education: whereas in the past we had an educational system that assumed the pyramid, now we have one that attempts to defy it (decrying as 'elitist' anyone who wants to assert the old common sense).

Note that this argument does not depend upon the development of a concept of 'intelligence'. The pyramid hypothesis remains equally plausible whether you thought there was one kind of intelligence or five or N, or that the concept of intelligence ought to be done away with altogether and replaced by different concepts for dealing with mental capacities. In any case, much of what is at stake here would not fall under the heading of 'intelligence' at all; I mean characteristics like concentration, determination and, above all, intellectual curiosity. The world is full of reasonably clever people who have no interest at all in the philosophical questions that lie at the heart of a traditional education. The quicker they can be freed from formal education to be clever in their own way, the better.

2. SELF-FULFILLING PROPHECY: 'Come on, Wayne! You know you can do it – you are going to score in the second half!' Thus do we all try to employ the positive aspect of

Robert Merton's concept of self-fulfilling prophecy. We say the market will rise and, if people believe us, it will rise. We tell people that our leader has power and, if they believe us, his power is increased. S-FP is an important phenomenon not only in understanding society, but also in controlling it. There are many educational circumstances in which you want to use it, to make people believe that they are going to achieve, because that belief is a necessary condition for their achieving.

But you can overdo it, and you must always be aware that the inverse phenomenon also exists – self-denying prophecy. The simplest version is when you tell somebody they are going to succeed and you cause them to fail because they become complacent. As a general rule, positive belief works in the short term, but scarcely in the medium term, and not at all in the long term. You can talk the markets up for a week, but you'd be stretching it to show an effect over a year, and certainly not over ten years. Boosting Wayne works well for the second half, but if he wants to be a professional he will need the talent and the character, and it would probably be better if you wound him up with a few insults to see what he's made of.

Unfortunately, our education system sees great merit in boosting people up to high levels of aspiration and to inflated views of their own abilities. In the long term, this must end in stress and disappointment, and therefore in unhappiness.

3. **INTERNALISATION**: By the end of *Tom Brown's Schooldays*, Tom has absorbed Dr Arnold's views on Christian Socialism and 'manly piety' to such a degree that it is fair to call him a disciple. There are even hints that the hero-worship of 'the Doctor' is a necessary step on the route to a full acceptance of Jesus Christ. The question raised by this is whether or not education should seek to be a moral training, whether it should inculcate values. There are two subsidiary forms of this question that concern rules and content. Should subjects be taught with a specifically ethical content? – the prime example of this being whether you should teach religion as if it were both true and prescriptive. And should the rules of the school be taken to be derived from some absolute

ideas of right and wrong? Or are they to be accepted as possibly arbitrary, but of aggregate benefit?

My own secondary education, as modelled in Scene 1 above, offered what was essentially the Hanoverian Solution to this question. You might have thought that the headmaster, who had been at Rugby before the First World War, was a direct cultural conduit back to Dr Arnold himself, and indeed some of his style did seem to be taken from *Tom Brown*. But the philosophical message of the institution as a whole was quite different: it suggested that ideological diversity – there were clearly Marxist, Tory, liberal and socialist masters, as well as religious believers and non-believers – was subjected to an overall sceptical utilitarianism. Boys were boys – bad little buggers – and occasionally had to be punished soundly so that order could be maintained and the benefits of education enjoyed. There was no relation between the views of individual masters and their willingness to punish, and no implication that punishment was anything more than a deterrent. Arbitrary punishment was practised: that is, punishing a randomly chosen individual when no culprit could be found, and it was (looking back) disproportionately the successful boys – good at sport and academic work – who suffered in this way. We did not respect this system or regard it as 'just' (it obviously wasn't), but we accepted it as necessary, like good Hanoverian subjects. And nearly everybody developed a considerable affection for the institution.

It is easy to run any human institution if you can make your subjects accept your own values – to 'internalise' them as sociologists often put it. This is an observation given great significance in the writings of Antonio Gramsci, who contrasts the crudeness of 'coercion' or 'dominance' with the subtlety of (ideological) 'hegemony'. Our situation was of crude, Roman-style dominance, reinforced by a perception of the need for government, of 'what the Romans did for us'.

The project that emerges from *Tom Brown* is of the public schools as staff colleges for a global Christian Socialist theocracy. If this wasn't the project of the Doctor himself, it is fairly explicitly that of one of his sons, Matthew.

Fortunately, this system of 'brain washing' – as a later generation would have called it – became thoroughly perverted. *Tom Brown* may be about a kind of religious crusade, but its thousands of imitators are about sporting rivalries and heroes, preoccupied with cricket, rugby and tradition. The public schools became staff colleges not of Christian Socialism, but of conservatism, imperialism and organised games. However, the Doctor's project lives on in many forms, through types of 'progressive' education. One current version is that schools should teach pupils the rights and duties of 'citizenship': it is to be hoped that young British subjects would be particularly disrespectful when faced with this project, whatever form it takes.

Quite by chance, I found myself in an unexpected version of the debate about values in education in the Creative Writing department of a Californian university. First-year students had been asked to write about the best day of their lives. One young man described how he and two friends from a small town in the San Joachim Valley had travelled to San Francisco to find a homosexual to beat up. Having located one and made sure that he and they were alone, they had proceeded to punch and kick him, savouring every blow. They had then relived the details on a thoroughly enjoyable journey home. Scarcely anything could have been more carefully designed to repel the staff on the creative writing course, but they all had to admit that it was an excellent piece of writing. It was clear, correct and fluent. More than that, out of a hundred pieces of writing, that was the one that everybody would remember. What they disagreed about was whether the immorality of the sentiments expressed could be said to detract from the quality of the writing. I liked to think that it was a pack of lies and that he had been making a point – a disrespectful point and an important one.

Our system of education may need more enthusiasm, more wisdom, more love and more of many other virtues; but it also needs a good deal more of the cold, clear acid of disrespect:

● There should be disrespect for the pupils: they should be freed from the notion that they are of any value or importance; they should be disabused of the idea that they have any kind of mission or destiny, and given to understand that they are a meaningless chemical accident with a wonderful opportunity.

● There should be disrespect for the parents, and recognition that the main way mums and dads fuck you up is by being stupid, ignorant and anti-intellectual.

● There should be disrespect for those who just aren't up to it, or who just aren't interested and who shouldn't be in the system at all.

● There should be disrespect on the part of pupils for the material put in front of them, generating the knowledge that the most important and exhilarating thing you can learn is how to spot and reject all the crap that is put in front of you.

'Based on a mistake'? Some 95 per cent of what they churn out in 'social studies' (85 per cent in the 'humanities') doesn't even get to that level: it says nothing coherent at all! It is discourse for discourse's sake, and its only possible use is to train people to spot and deal with the nonsense they will be surrounded with all their lives.

● There should be raging contempt for the educational administrators and 'researchers' who have got us where we are.

● In a 'multicultural society' it is important that pupils should be taught to disrespect *all* the component cultures.

7

RESPECT FOR HUMANS, ANIMALS ... EVEN OIKS?

A utilitarian must accept that, in principle, every sentient being must have account taken of it in every public decision. That means you must be *considered*, included in the calculation. It does not mean that you won't *rightly* be tortured for information, eaten or have an atomic bomb dropped on you if the calculation of the aggregate so requires. Of course, it is important to realise that no ethical system can actually offer you any worthwhile guarantee against these things; but utilitarianism is unique in making it clear from the outset that it might be *right* to torture you.

Thus 'consideration' does not constitute a 'right' in any normal sense, and certainly not according to Dworkin's analogy of a 'trump' that can be played to thwart the aggregate.[32] One of the most consistent themes of both scepticism and utilitarianism is the opposition to 'human' or 'natural' rights: natural and prescriptible rights, universal rights 'taken seriously' so to speak, were dismissed by Jeremy Bentham as 'nonsense on stilts'.[33] In any case, declarations of rights never seem to have done the target audience much good: the declaration of rights by the French National Assembly in 1791 (including the right to life) was followed by the guillotining of more than 4,000 people, and the United States Bill of Rights of the same year was held to be compatible with the institution of slavery for a further 73 years. Rights enthusiasts will find some pretty little rights in the Soviet Constitution of 1936. In short, natural or human rights (as opposed to specific privileges acquired under a well-established legal system) are quite useless to honest men and women, and we should expect more malice from those who claim to believe in them than from those who do not. The stronger case is to say that they usually benefit only criminals and lawyers.

Thus utilitarianism offers no intrinsic 'respect' for human beings, but only the untrumplike, uncashable consideration due to the sentient. Bentham and his successors have always made it clear that consideration is also due to creatures other than humans – the question being not thought, but feeling. However, the nature of pain and pleasure is changed entirely and made much more profound by the existence of a conscious mind, and the consequent capacities for the extension of pleasure and pain through reflection, anticipation, satisfaction, etc. In the case of pain, this is well put by the poet Robert Burns, here talking about the mouse whose nest he destroyed with a plough in November 1785:

> Still thou art blest, compar'd wi' me!
> The present only toucheth thee;
> But, Och! I backward cast my e'e,
> On prospects drear!
> An' forward, tho' I cannot see,
> I guess and fear![34]

The same is true of pleasure, and the range of sentience can be considered to be much greater in human beings, who alone can experience love and loss, sorrow and satisfaction; there is no need to invoke John Stuart Mill's conception of 'higher' pleasures in order to justify a vastly greater weight for humans over other creatures. This is not simply biological chauvinism, because, if another species showed the same combination of consciousness and feeling, it would become ethically 'human' – whatever it was biologically. This hardly challenges our concept of humanity, since there is no other such species; chimpanzees – the species that probably comes nearest – are so lacking in numbers (largely on account of human activity) that we could easily afford to privilege them as ourselves.

It follows that human beings are only equal *a priori*. 'Each is to count for one', says Bentham, but as the consideration proceeds, they become increasingly unequal. Utilitarians like to play the game about who should be thrown out of the hot-air balloon to prevent it from crashing. This pastime is rather problematic from the perspective of other ethical systems. Given the combined calculation of their effects on others and their capacity for sentience, bright, charming 20-year-olds are worth more – much more – than cantankerous 80-year-olds suffering from Alzheimer's; and they ought to be treated as more worthy. Only the dogmas of theism and humanism could prevent us from seeing this. Actually, people who make decisions in our society (I mean here the United Kingdom in the 21st century), whether in the National Health Service or the Treasury, generally make them as utilitarians, but try to avoid explicitness.

In the light of this philosophical approach, it is interesting to consider the nature of 'society' – and perhaps 'the nation' and other collective abstractions. Contemporary writing, particularly by people who describe themselves as 'fogeys' (or who are described by others as such), melds two important themes: moral decay (generally) and the underclass. Probably not since the mid-19th century, when the trip to Manchester (and the subsequent book or article) was almost a defining condition of being an intellectual, has discussion about the lower strata of society been as intense as it is now: Marx, Engels, Mill, Dickens, Disraeli, Faucher and Kay-Shuttleworth were among those who made the trip then, while Elizabeth Gaskell actually lived there. In our own times, we have Christie Davies, Francis Gilbert, Theodore Dalrymple, Andrew Wilson *et al.* discussing a syndrome of violence, drunkenness, drug use, promiscuous sex, marital breakdown, etc. In terms of a society based on mutual respect, the observed phenomena certainly throw up a challenge, and the government has come to label this area of challenge and response the 'respect agenda'; I note that one of the ministers responsible for implementing the 'respect agenda' is a former personal student of mine – a very nice man, chiefly notable for having managed that rare feat of failing his first-year university exams twice.

So, 'they' show no respect for 'us' or for 'society' or 'the community', and we have no respect for them. 'They' do like to use the word 'respect', but usually appear to understand it amorally, in terms of crude coercive power, the respect for the street gang leader whose threats have credibility. 'Their' existence in this form is shocking, partly because it seems to be a reversion from the kind of harmony and conformity we expected to follow from the creation of the welfare state. The similarities with the 1840s' debate about the 'Condition of England' are considerable: concern for the moral welfare of the lower classes, combined with personal physical fear of them; a desire to 'incorporate' them (we now talk of 'inclusion') into the respectable mainstream. But there are important differences: the lower class of 1845 was an incipient majority, a political unknown that raised Karl Marx's 'spectre' of revolution. The current underclass poses no political threat, is politically inert and a long way from being any kind of majority. Figures are ambiguous and elusive, but the underclass is probably between 5 per cent and 20 per cent of the population, depending on criteria, though the matter is considerably confused by some underclass behaviour being much more widespread. As they grow up, most young people are involved in 'binge drinking' at some stage, for example. There is a good deal of 'slumming it', though the way out of this is generally quite easy and inexpensive.

One author who is mysteriously absent from most discussion of these social problems is the American sociologist, Edward Banfield. Set alongside his analysis, the arguments both of the Left and of the supposedly conservative 'fogeys' begin to look remarkably similar. In the 1950s, Banfield researched what he called the 'amoral familism' of Sicily, and in the 1960s turned his attention to the 'urban decay' and 'multiple deprivation' of the American cities.[35] His analysis is in terms of four classes: upper, middle, working and lower. But what is unconventional is that these classes are defined by their time horizons: the upper class is dynastic, the middle class plans for their whole lives, while the lower classes concern themselves largely with almost immediate gratification. Thus, it does not really matter what other people think of you or what obstacles they put in your way; it is your fundamental attitudes that determine your fate. This is a very similar account of the working of society to that found in Samuel

Smiles' *Self-Help* or in Warwick Deeping's best-selling 1925 novel, *Sorrell and Son* (which is also remarkably similar to the 2006 film *The Pursuit of Happyness* – written by Steve Conrad, directed by Gabriele Muccino and starring Will Smith). It is a view of society that the Left has always found particularly exasperating: witness George Orwell's loathing of Warwick Deeping.

The implication is that change can only be internal to the individual, and that governments are among the least likely agents or even catalysts of real change. For the most part (and this is a judgement on early forms of poverty programmes) they make things worse, often by adding to a culture of 'dependency'. Banfield's immediate practical response to the underclass is cartographical: get a map, find out where they hang out, don't go there... This is hardly an option for Dalrymple, who operates as a psychiatrist in a prison and the cheaper parts of the city; nor for Gilbert, who has set himself the task of researching yobbery. Generally, I suppose, it is easier in the USA, where the locations of the underclass are fairly specific in a very large country, than it is in Britain, which is much smaller and where you are likely to see brawling, binge drinking and drug abuse even in 'idyllic' villages.

But I think there is a good deal to be learned from Banfield's analysis and from his insistence that the condition that is attracting so much attention is, to borrow the traditional metaphor of the body politic, less a cancer than a minor viral infection. One of the most intellectually objectionable features of the revived 'Condition of England' debate is its persistent collectivism. Take, for example, Theodore Dalrymple, whose recent essays are collected under the heading *Our Culture, What's Left of It*.[36] These essays are about various conditions of society, but are much concerned with evil, the underclass and the arts. I hope it is fair to say that there is an underlying theme, which contrasts a European tradition of sensitivity, refinement and ethical restraint with the vulgarity and moral decay observable in contemporary society. The genre is 'social criticism'. It is not ethical philosophy: we are never told whether or not Dalrymple bases his moral standards on a fully fledged belief in deontology (which I will equate, for the moment, with a belief in absolute rules, however derived, that must be obeyed whatever the consequences). Similarly, when Christie Davies bemoans the loss of a 'protestant' identity in England and Wales, it sometimes seems as if he merely enjoys the consequences of being among Protestants, rather than thinking there is something worth believing in Protestantism.

Social criticism is the product of a mental habit that entered our culture in the 19th century: it might be called the 'sociological mentality'. It combines description and explanatory models with tacit or covert explanation of human behaviour and institutions. It entirely avoids properly constructed ethical argument, with premises and conclusions. Marx and Engels never argue for Communism: they never tell you that God wants you to be a Communist, or that it is demonstrable that we would, taken as a whole, be happier under Communism (which would be genuine ethical arguments, broadly considered). Instead they employ the hyper-typical move of the social critic and mix up ethics with science: they tell you that Communism is inevitable. The trouble is that, in the ocean of words, there are thousands of gallons of social criticism for every pint of clear ethical philosophy, but social criticism is an entirely inadequate substitute for ethics. And the reasons are fairly obvious: few people like clear and logical thinking, and even fewer like to go where it takes them.

But it is the collectivism of this form of writing that must be treated with the most immediate suspicion: 'Our culture'. Let me describe my most recent Christmas – my first as a sexagenarian – or at least the public events that were involved. We went to a carol concert, a Music Hall event put on by the local dramatic society, the seasonal blockbuster at the Royal Shakespeare Company, a ball in a newly designed tropical greenhouse, two football matches and a race meeting. The technical achievements of these events certainly varied, but they were all particularly well attended and well behaved. 'Our' culture seemed to be doing rather well. Somewhere in the town, somebody would have been vomiting over themselves, somebody would have been injecting themselves with an addictive drug and somebody would have been sustaining some nasty injuries in a fight. But it is a strange mentality (and certainly not a utilitarian one) which thinks that the one set of phenomena somehow negates the other. Part of this implication, though, may have to do with the way in which publishers present books, rather than what authors write in them. In the case of successful 'serious' books, there are many more people who can cite the title than have actually read the book. Martin Wiener's *English Culture and the Decline of the Industrial Spirit* was actually written (and reads as if it was written) with the word *Containment* instead of *Decline*. Perhaps the idea that there's not much left of 'our' culture was foisted on the author, because it is not particularly clear from the essays. On the other hand, Francis Gilbert seems to believe that there are yobs everywhere, in government and in the City, as well as on the streets. But he gives the impression of being so prissy that – to adopt Erewhonian assumptions for a moment – he should never have chosen to come to this planet in the first place.

Mrs Thatcher has been much reviled for the most famous piece of philosophy ever to grace *Woman's Own*: 'There's no such thing as society, but only individuals and families.' But it's a commonplace enough remark, and, in a sense, the thought is true of all abstractions. There is also no such thing as democracy or liberty or virtue – in some sense. But it is particularly important to grasp the senses in which society does not exist. First and foremost, it is not an entity. Entities have continuities and thing-like limitations. They cannot go in opposite directions at the same time, and they can be said to be doing well or badly. Societies can go in totally opposite directions at the same time. In both Britain and the USA, at the time of writing, the lower and working classes are getting fatter, while the middle and upper classes are getting thinner. It's getting to the point that you can tell somebody's social class from a quarter of a mile away with half-decent eyesight! The average may remain the same; but the average (which is like society and, in a sense, *is* society) doesn't (in a sense) exist. In 30 years of watching football and teaching in universities, I have seen behaviour become markedly more genteel. Students do not storm over to administration buildings and 'occupy' them for three weeks, as they did 30 years ago. Nor do they shout 'fucking crap' at you during your very first lecture, as happened to a contemporary of mine; they are extremely polite. (If it had happened to me...) Football crowds stand obediently through one-minute (and even two-minute) silences nowadays, whereas 30 years ago these were invariably punctuated by obscene chants. They even 'respect' no-smoking stadiums in traditional heavy-industry areas like Middlesbrough. I would not, of course, wish to infer that society *per se* has 'improved'.

It is also important to note that society as such cannot be a moral entity. You cannot owe it anything. Unlike with the cricket club, you do not (*Erewhon* apart) choose to join it, and you can form no obligations to it. What, anyway, are its boundaries? Do I live in English society? Or British? European? Western? Global?

I confess that I share with James I (of England and VI of Scotland) a peculiarly intense irritation with the poet and divine John Donne – or at least with one of his best known works, the 'Meditation XVII'. James, who had bullied Donne into taking orders in the established Church, complained that his sermons were 'like the peace of God; they pass all understanding'. My complaint is that this particular meditation licenses sloppy and sentimental thinking about society. Its most famous lines are:

> No man is an island, entire of itself; every man is a piece of the continent, a part of the main. & Any man's death diminishes me, because I am involved in mankind; and therefore never send to know for whom the bell tolls; it tolls for thee.[37]

The first sentiment is merely vague: of course, we are interconnected in some respects. The second is much worse. Whereas it is natural that one should feel enormous sorrow at some deaths, there could not be a worse prescription than to increase this sorrow beyond its natural or minimal boundaries. Approximately 3,000 people die in the United Kingdom every day!

I have never been closer to putting my foot through a television set than when watching Humphrey Atkins, then Secretary of State for Northern Ireland, on American television, quoting 'Meditation XVII' after the death in 1981 of the IRA hunger striker, Bobby Sands. The implication of a world in which enough people could swallow that crap was painful. By way of a palliative, I fondly remembered the first departmental chairman I worked under. He was 40 years older than me. He had spent most of his life in Oxford and Whitehall, and therefore knew a disproportionate number of 'the great and the good'. Mid-morning, he would sometimes call me in to light a celebratory cigarette as he looked at the obituaries. Tapping a photograph of the deceased, he would say: 'Now he was a *real* shit.' Ask for whom the bell tolls – and then enjoy if appropriate; you wouldn't care if they did the same to you.

This argument would not be complete without an angry nod in the direction of the late Lord Devlin. In *The Enforcement of Morals*, he combined a rather crude populism with elements of natural law theory in the Catholic tradition.[38] In the 1960s, he was the best-known opponent of the moves that were under way to remove state regulation of sexual matters, as justified by the contemporary expressions of Millian liberalism in the writings of Herbert Hart and in the deliberations of the Home Office committee, under Sir John (later Lord) Wolfenden, which had reported in 1957. The populism consisted of an assertion that part of the role of law was enforcement of popular prejudice, a touching posh lawyer's faith that 'the man on the Clapham omnibus' shares his own prejudices, which derive from some ancient religious law; looking back, this conjures up a vision of London that certainly does not exist now – if indeed it ever did. If there still is a Clapham omnibus and if it has three-seaters, there is probably a lesbian feminist sitting in the middle, with a Muslim fundamentalist on one side and a gay rights activist on the other! No point in kicking a man when he's down, though, and Patrick Devlin's image of English society is now merely quaint. But some of his social theory is not, especially his belief that society has a 'moral fabric' that defines it: thus his most notorious argument, that legalising homosexuality would lead to the breakdown of marriage. To be fair to Devlin, the two have coincided – which should be of some concern to those who believe in society in its strong sense.

My concern here is to debunk the tradition of social criticism, of which much contemporary debate is a part – certainly including that surrounding the government's 'Respect Agenda'. I would not, however, like any reader to think that I lack human sympathy. I have every sympathy for members of the underclass. If my father had disappeared; if my mother was inarticulate and bad-tempered; if I had no money; if I was made to go to a disorderly and pointless institution called a school, which offered me no solutions to any of my problems – then yes, I would want to destroy some property. And if the best I could hope for ('success') was to go to some dismal hole now called a 'university'; to spend three years getting into debt and recycling trivial bits of information in order to be able to put the letters 'BA' after my name; to get a tedious job that involved a three-hour commute every day; and to be obliged to pay off an even bigger debt called a mortgage – then yes, I would want to get blind drunk (at the very least), and yes, I might well end up giving somebody a smack.

As it is, I am an educated, comfortably-off chap who has had everything handed him on a plate; who doesn't need to work; and who is as 'free' as a human being could ever be... and *still* I want to put bricks through the windows of four-wheel drive vehicles and write FUCK OFF on the wall of the Town Hall.

But, to insist again on the distinction that was once so easily made but that now seems so difficult for most people to make, sympathy isn't the point. In the debate about football hooliganism, I always felt that the participants (in the debate) really didn't have a clue, because they had no desire to be hooligans themselves. *'Tout comprendre, c'est tout pardonner'* said the *saloniste* Madame De Staël. Nothing could be less correct: to understand all is to know that only severe coercion, harshness to a purpose – what John Rawls called 'telishment' – will do.

8

PSYCHOWANNABES

Harold Lasswell's *Psychopathology and Politics*, originally published in 1930, is a young man's book in the sense that it is obsessed with a single, all-explaining idea; it was written, when the author was in his twenties, during and after a trip to Europe.[39] The central argument is Freudian, and the writings of Sigmund Freud, though not treated uncritically, are seen as the basis for the answers to all important questions, both scientific and artistic. The essence of the argument is that political action is the displacement of individual and *abnormal* psychological conditions onto public objects. The conditions of being an 'agitator', an 'administrator' or a 'theorist' have their origins in such conditions as 'Oedipus' and 'castration' complexes and the sublimation of homosexual desire, though there is no standard or categorisable relation between cause and effect. (That is, it is not the case that agitation is *always* linked to homosexual urges, or a yearning for administrative power to a castration complex, etc.) The causal conditions themselves have their origins in childhood traumas and deprivations. Thus, although the extent of the term 'politician' is problematical, Lasswell is able to say that the condition of being a politician is a deviant one.

Most of the book, which is over 300 pages long in its later editions, consists of case studies, in which we learn, to give an abstracted and contrived example, how N's nocturnal emissions while sharing a bed with his father led him to become a fiercely puritanical and radical agitator. They are at best suggestive, and it is a pity that they are extended to the exclusion of considerations of the conceptual and ethical problems of the theory. One obvious conceptual problem is the limit of the idea of what constitutes political ambition. A version of the answer is that it is a 'power drive'; but sometimes what people actually want is not 'power', but something more akin to acclaim, status or recognition. 'Politics' also seems to lack boundaries: one's psychosis might drive one in (more or less) the same way to the school, the university or the newspaper office, as much as to Parliament. The obvious conceptual trap here is that everybody who does anything at all is deviant, and if a society consisted wholly – or even largely – of 'normal' people, it would be running on an ambition deficit, or even an action deficit. It is not at all clear from Lasswell what kinds of human action would not be psychopathological in origin, though 'sculpture' is cited in one case study.

For a utilitarian, the ethical problem is rather different from that facing those whose moral outlook is religious or deontological, as utilitarians judge actions on their consequences, and there may be many circumstances in which it is better to be a 'psychopath' than to be 'normal'. The only ethical distinction implied by Lasswell's psychological distinction is that 'normals' are less significant than psychopaths, who are likely to do either more harm or more good. Hitler's wickedness may have been psychopathological in origin, but so were the qualities that Churchill brought to bear as the main agent of his defeat. Churchill defined himself as a psychopath in this sense during a conversation with Lord Halifax, which the latter reported to James Lees-Milne, who later recorded it in his diary. It is late 1938, and it has become clear that the German government has broken the Munich agreement on Czechoslovak independence:

> After serious discussion Lord Cecil said, 'Well, Winston, things are desperate. I feel twenty years older.' Churchill replied equally seriously, 'Yes, Bob. Things are desperate. I feel twenty years younger.'
> – and these words convinced Harold that Churchill was a great man. They convince me that Churchill enjoys war.[40]

T. E. Lawrence, Florence Nightingale and General Charles Gordon were three national heroes who were also – if the distinction means anything – psychopaths, and in every case their condition had a clear and painful sexual dimension that would probably be taken by Freudians as its origin. Yet their worth as people, and the extent to which we should approve their actions, seems genuinely debatable in each case. Thus, even if you accept the psychopathology theory of politics, you have to start all over again with ethics, distinguishing dysfunctional psychopathology from functional.

However, and despite these fundamental flaws, I think Lasswell's argument has considerable merit (as does the very limited and dated genre of psycho-politics that can be put alongside it, e.g. in the writings of Nathan Leites). At the very least, it asks important questions. Other theories of politics in general – and of democracy in particular – shut themselves off from questions about what makes people rulers rather than ruled, elected rather than electors. It is as if it is just a given or, as in the liberal theory of taste, a randomly dealt desire. Or public spirit, sheer republican virtue persuading good men from their tilling, like Cincinnatus in Rome's hour of need. But we must at least entertain the hypothesis that politicians might be more like Coriolanus than Cincinnatus, bullying Mummy's boys, whose careers are driven by deep needs, the effects of which are going to be felt by us. In other words, we both need and lack a theory of ambition and a prescription for how to deal with ambition, how to limit it, channel it and so on.

I will attempt to sketch a theory of ambition by outlining the distinctions between three 'ideal types' of human being. The point here is not, as it would be for Lasswell and other Freudians, to illustrate the difference between their origins and development, but to show the ethical significance of their difference from a utilitarian standpoint:

1. THE AUTONOMY-SEEKER (henceforth 'aut'). The aut wants to be as independent as possible in as many respects as possible. Of course, the autonomy of the hermit is not a desirable condition for most people, so there are goods, in exchange for which most of us will sacrifice considerable autonomy. These are, principally, love, marriage and family. But auts want to get up in the morning on their own property, feeling healthy, and to ponder what they might do today and how, if at all, they should spend their money. An aut is completely successful when he or she can ask, over a glass of champagne, 'What shall we do tomorrow, darling?'

2. THE ATTENTION-SEEKER (henceforth 'att'). Given the conditions that constitute perfection for the aut, the att would fret and scheme and make phone calls. He or she prefers having too many emails to having none. Gratification only comes with the appeasement of the gnawing sense of inadequacy that is at the core of their being. It normally comes in the form of 'fame' or 'celebrity'.

Atts have a positive utilitarian value, because they entertain us. But they are also a utilitarian problem in the aggregate, because the goods that they want are what Fred Hirsch called 'positional' goods. A predominantly aut world is thus capable of general happiness far above the level possible in a predominantly att world. And the proportion of atts seems to be increasing, whether because of the mass media, or dysfunctional families, or for some other reason that does not really matter to my argument. Thus one of the most serious problems for contemporary happiness, illustrated by the frequency with which Andy Warhol's 1968 statement is quoted: 'In the future everyone will be world famous for 15 minutes.' (Incidentally, the arithmetic doesn't work: there is only really time for everyone in a population about the size of the Republic of Ireland's to be *uniquely* famous. But, since the evidence that you are actually famous is bound to be merely circumstantial, perhaps we can get by on combinations of local fame, shared fame and illusory fame.)

Thus, also, the proliferation of means by which anybody can aspire to be famous (that is, without connections, education, talent and so on). The best example here is 'reality' television, which can make you famous for just wanting to be famous, or for being particularly quarrelsome or stupid. These means are generally a Good Thing, since they serve as a *reductio ad absurdum* of fame, detaching it from ideas of success and status, and thus helping to undermine something that is, in the aggregate, causing unhappiness.

It is important to accept that atts are normally harmless in themselves, possessed of an honest neediness that is pathetic rather than threatening. In the aggregate, their predominance is harmful to the general happiness; but individual atts do not threaten the happiness of individual auts. The spirit of the att is often best captured when they experience complete gratification and abandon all deceit. Thus Oscar acceptance speeches are a rich vein of insight into the condition. Witness that of the actress Sally Field in 1984. It has been much misquoted, but here is the original:

> I haven't had an orthodox career and I've wanted more than anything to have your respect. The first time I didn't feel it, but this time I feel it, and I can't deny the fact that you like me! Right now, you like me![41]

(Autonomy, of course, would involve not giving a damn!)

3. THE POWER-SEEKER (henceforth 'pow'). Lasswell confuses atts and pows, but from a utilitarian point of view they are entirely different. Atts are often happy if you say something like: 'My, you're a pretty girl' (which, as a utilitarian, you ought always to do, unless there is a very good reason for not doing so). But pows offer a much more direct threat to your well-being. A pow can achieve gratification only by threatening you and making you fearful of him or her. There is an important sense in which the rapist, the serial killer and the Chancellor of the Exchequer are all the same kind of psychopath – though I must, of course, insist that there *can* be good Chancellors, but only bad rapists and serial killers. Of course, in a rational-legal society in Weberian terms, this threat does not come in the naked form in which the Bold Bad Sultan offers it. It is displaced, as Lasswell rightly points out, onto public objects. Thus the pow is going to coerce you into 'caring' about things that you would be better off not caring about; he is going to raise your consciousness or insist on your duty to the company. He is always going to stress the primacy of the collective over the individual, and he is usually going to be *étatiste* in one form or another. Pows will always exist, but we ought to judge societies in terms of the number of pows and the extent to which the society is institutionally capable of mitigating power-seeking. In order to understand more fully the subtlety and importance of this judgement, and in the spirit of Freud and Lasswell, we must now proceed to a case study.

THE STORY OF PROFESSOR A

A was born in a Midlands industrial town in the late 1940s. His father was a skilled worker at the local carpet factory, and his mother was a nurse who, after he was born, worked part time. Two years after he was born, his mother gave birth to a daughter. Mr and Mrs A were respectable people who had owned their own semi-detached house since they had married in 1939, and they were prospering as A grew up. However, all was not quite what it seemed in the A household. A's father had spent more than six years abroad with the 8th Army, during which time Mrs A had entered into what would now be called a 'relationship' with another man. Although Mr and Mrs A stayed together, there were considerable tensions. A felt that his father was always resentful of him, and that his sister was more loved by his parents. He once accidentally saw his father having sex quite brutally with his mother, who was bent over the end of the bed.

Nevertheless, A grew up fairly normal and successful. He was good at school and, although he was relatively small and had far from perfect vision, he played left-back in the school football team and managed to hold onto that position in the age-group teams when he went on to grammar school. In both schools he had a small circle of friends, with whom he spent most of his time. But when he was 17, the family tensions came to a head and his father left home to live with a female colleague in a house that he had inherited, though Mr and Mrs A never divorced. A was upset and his 'A' levels suffered. As a result, he was not admitted to a university, but went instead to a polytechnic. He was, though, a star student there, and was awarded a first-class degree, after which he received a government grant to study for a Master's degree at the University of Metropolis. After demonstrating further success there, he received funding to do a doctorate, and before he had finished the doctorate he was awarded a lectureship at Littlehampton University. This precipitated his marriage to Sarah, a fellow student, who abandoned her own doctoral plans and bore him two children within two years.

The early years of his professional life were a struggle for A. His doctorate was 'referred', although he was eventually awarded it after a further 18 months' work. He had difficulty in getting articles published in academic journals. His teaching suffered from the other pressures on him, including those of bringing up a young family. But all of this changed dramatically just after his mid-thirties: he spotted a fashionable method and a promising topic, and was able to turn out a book and several articles in a little over a year. None of this was either original or well written, but the absence of those qualities was no problem. The book won a prize and, because the field had followers in government, he was awarded a large research grant. His university quickly followed this up with a promotion to Senior Lecturer. But that is where they made their mistake, for, after secret negotiations and the offer of a high salary, A announced his move to a 'chair' at the up-and-coming University of Barchester.

He took the opportunity to abandon Sarah and the children in Littlehampton (they didn't want to leave, anyway). His new companion was Jane, a former graduate student of his from a wealthy background. His chief complaint about Sarah, he tells people, is that she didn't take his career seriously enough.

Professor A, for the first time in his life, is a wealthy and powerful man. He has the respect he craves and that he thinks he deserves. We can be happy for him – though less so for his deserted wife and children. And less so, too, for his new colleagues. He is not going to mature into a kindly old don, beloved of colleagues and students alike. His appointment at Barchester is entirely due to the introduction of the 'Research Assessment Exercise', a device whereby all individuals and departments in universities are given a score for their contribution to 'research': huge amounts of money and status depend on that score. Professor A is a 'research professor', whose job it is to get productivity up. He is a 'manager', a 'leader'. This means he has to frighten some people into resigning or retiring. In more promising cases, he sets targets and offers help in finding 'outlets' and winning grants. He cultivates the younger members and some of the graduate students: they find it prudent under his patronage to act as disciples. There is no doubt that Professor A enjoys all this. He talks about 'modernising' his department and dragging his colleagues 'kicking and screaming' into a more competitive era. He proudly tells people that he never meets an undergraduate, the implication being that he is far too important to do so. He takes peculiar pleasure in 'shaking up' his Oxbridge-educated colleagues, who, he thinks, have for years been resting on their laurels. He has discovered the aphrodisiac of power: secretaries and young academics laugh at his jokes and accept his drinks invitations, even though, among themselves, they say he is 'creepy'.

At one time, under old Professor B, the department was rather a happy place. People went about their business and took a pride in the quality of their teaching and the smooth running of the department. Only about a third of them did anything significant that came to the notice of the outside world, but Professor B's view was that people should only publish if they had something to say, and that, for many people, ideas took some time to mature. The department was a place where people acted with great autonomy in running their courses and developing their scholarly interests. It was also very communal, coming together happily for social events organised around exams and visiting speakers: good fences make good neighbours.

Now it is an utterly miserable place, where a letter from a journal editor can seem to make or break a career, and where young women take refuge in older colleagues' offices, sobbing with the sheer stress of it all; where secretaries resign their jobs because they find themselves feeling sick in the car park when they look up at the building that houses the department; where young academics on short-term contracts work 12-hour days when they should be at home with their babies. And what do we have to compensate us for all this misery? Additional academic articles that gave no pleasure to write and that will not be read. Professor A is not the sole cause of this misfortune, but he is the principal local agent of it.

Professor A is a jumped-up dreary little cad. This raises two kinds of question. I do not think even the most wildly optimistic social engineer would hope to produce a world in which dreary little cads did not exist. But we may be able to stop them jumping up. In other words, there is the psychological question: how did he come to have the psychopathic drives that cause so much misery? And then there is the ethical-political question: what are we going to do about it?

The psychological question does not matter and cannot be answered. I have (to use another Weberian expression) constructed a 'plausible story' to suggest *why* Professor A might have become as he is, but who really knows what combination of his many deprivations caused him to be the way he is? And who cares? When it comes to responsibility, the war was clearly an important event in the story. So can we blame Hitler? Or the Kaiser? Psychology is an impossible exercise – unless, perhaps, it is allowed to conduct control experiments on an infinitely large number of people. Freudianism offers a few insights into extreme cases, but does not help us with the numerous ordinary psychopaths who surround us.

The ethical-political question, however, must be answered. How did we come to create a context in which cads could thrive? To produce anything so obviously insane as the Research Assessment Exercise? The answer is both dreadful and fascinating; it lies in the Sovietisation of western society that has occurred since the demise of the Soviet Union, and that was partly legitimised by that demise, often under the offensively inaccurate name of 'neo-liberalism'. What it *should* be called is neo-Libermanism after Evsei Liberman, the reforming economist who tried to make something of the Soviet economy after the death of Stalin. In order to do so, he recommended forms of competition between factories that were devised and manipulated by the state: aims and objectives, naming and shaming, league tables and assessment committees – all are Libermanisms, now all too familiar to us. If you are going to have *étatiste* institutions, at least let them be relaxed and corrupt, encouraging an atmosphere in which good chaps rather than psychopaths will thrive.

But if this is an impossible prescription, what we can do is nurture a culture of suspicion and contempt for ambition – or, at least, for those forms of ambition that involve power-seeking. The fundamental ethical law is that those who want respect should receive contempt – just for wanting it. Politicians always argue that this happens far too much already; that there is a kind of 'respect deficit', a 'culture of cynicism' induced by the media, satirists and comedians. We are entitled to ask in return what politicians have ever done for honest citizens? Even Mrs Thatcher's attempts to 'roll back the state' mostly turned into a process of Libermanisation.

There are two further arguments in political theory that should be invoked to put the 'respect deficit' into its proper context. The first comes from Walter Bagehot's *The English Constitution,* and invokes the distinction between 'efficient' and 'dignified' elements of the constitution.[42] The former wield authority and make decisions, while the latter accrue authority and attract loyalty. The principal efficient element is the Cabinet and the principal dignified element is the monarch. In no sense and under no circumstances ought politicians to be respected; monarchs should be respected in one sense, and might be in the other. That is, they have a right to our formal respect as the embodiment of our collective identity and history, and, because they are not self-selected, they *might* be worthy of our spontaneous moral respect.

The other important argument comes from Joseph Schumpeter's *Capitalism, Socialism and Democracy*.[43] It concerns the 'division of labour' between the elected and the electors, in a system that is democratic at least in the minimal sense of allowing a regular mechanism for the rejection of governments. Schumpeter is an extremist on this question (as he had a right to be, being a refugee who had observed what happened to German and Austrian democracy): he is even against the petitioning of parliamentarians. The important distinction here is roughly that made by Frederick the Great, when he said that he had a compact with his people: they could say what they liked, while he could do what he liked. It is important in this argument to distinguish 'speech' from 'action'. This distinction always has been important to liberals, and it is sometimes quite difficult – thus John Stuart Mill's distinction between expressing a view on the Corn Laws in a journal and expressing the same view to a drunken mob outside a corn merchant's house. But technology has made this distinction a good deal easier, since we now have a plethora of means of expressing ideas and arguments in circumstances that allow others a genuine choice as to whether or not they want to hear us. 'Protest', on the other hand, is not speech, and governments should be allowed to deal with pickets, road-barricaders and port-blockers as harshly as they think fit. That is not because citizens ought to respect governments, but because there is a division of labour: government, like waste disposal, must go on. Provided we have free speech, we probably have more to fear from the mob than from the government.

9

RESPECT FOR THE ARTIST

La Cappella Sistina – the Sistine Chapel. It may be February, but the tourist season now lasts all year, and Rome's most famous chapel is as full as a football ground. I am part of a party of Catholic head teachers (believe it or not), and when I manage to find a seat it is next to the youngest in the party, the headmistress of a primary school. We look to our left, to where the whole 'altar' wall is taken up by Michelangelo Buonarroti's painting of the *Last Judgement*. 'Isn't it magnificent?' she breathes, rhetorically.

Actually, it's rubbish: a grandiose, gaudy piece of agit-prop-cliché, painted by a sculptor (as he regarded himself) who didn't want to do it, who didn't believe in it, but who was given political and financial incentives to do the job. It was a propaganda piece painted between 1535/36 and 1541, as part of the burgeoning ideological war between Catholics and Protestants. The artist amused himself by including some fairly explicit genitalia, which had to be covered up by Daniele da Volterra (*il Braghettone*, 'the trouser man'). When it was restored, between 1981 and 1994, there was considerable controversy. People were shocked by the '*gelati*' colours: frankly, if the word 'gaudy' has a meaning, this is it. It was argued that Michelangelo must have meant it to be seen through a patina of oil and smoke. Even so, my companion would have had Goethe on her side. He said that, without seeing it, ' ... one can form no appreciable idea of what one man is capable of achieving'.

The issue here is not really my opinion of a particular work of art. Rather, what is interesting is the sense of reverence that art engenders. I know, from experience and experiment, that if you tell a Catholic headmistress that transubstantiation, the Trinity and the Immaculate Conception are all nonsense, you will not cause offence. You are merely being predictable, and it is known that there is a case for what you say. But 'diss' the Sistine Chapel and you may, even in these hardened days, cause shock. Reverence goes beyond particular works of art to the ideas of 'Art' and 'the Arts' in general. Art justifies immorality: this was famously true of the assumptions accepted by the *Lady Chatterley* trial in 1961, but it has also been true of a host of 'artists', self-ascribed or publicly accepted, whose art has justified their bad behaviour. One musician of my generation used, as his chief item of persuasive seduction of other people's wives, the suggestion that making love with them would improve his artistic performance. In art lie our contemporary hopes of finding the profound, the spiritual, the immortal. Artistic things are the humanist equivalent of holy things. People yearn for contact with them. But they are also desperate to contribute. At dawn, in the Valley of the Kings in Upper Egypt, 400 coaches disgorge their passengers, who then start to snap away – even if this means having to thrust their cameras into the air and press the button without knowing exactly what the camera is pointing at. The BBC abandoned poetry competitions because they made it snow poetry: the Corporation simply couldn't cope with the response. From graffiti vandals to repetitive photographers, to wives who offer their own adulterous contribution to artistic production – the urge to spray one's creative urine on the territory is not to be underestimated. It is, perhaps, the sense that being an artist makes you exist in a way that is more durable, higher or more real. (The analogy with religion need not be laboured.)

We cannot completely ignore the question of what 'art' is or what 'the arts' are. Given how valuable and important people assume they are, it is a category in which people are quite passionate about what is included and what excluded; and this passion can combine with intrinsic paradox to generate hours of harmless fun. Are cars art? Are graffiti? Confectionery wrappers? What about art that refuses to be art? Le Corbusier's insistence on 'functionalism' eschews 'decoration' in building: do 'modernist' buildings thereby cease to be art? Or should we treat them as updated, clever, 'relevant' art? Like Jackson Pollock's 'Jack the Dripper' paintings, which can be simulated by a chimpanzee – and which can only be authenticated by a chemical analysis of the paint. Which brings us on to 'concept' art: Tracey Emin's bed and Damien Hirst's pickled sheep. The paradox is that anti-art is, at a certain point, the true art. Who cares?

The answer I used to present to young people, even when I myself was young, is based on an essay by W. B. Gallie.[44] It is that 'Art', like 'Democracy' and 'a Christian Life', is an 'essentially contested concept'. Which means that part of its meaning consists of a disagreement about its meaning – *essential* disagreement, which cannot be resolved and which remains part of the meaning. How does that differ from 'radically confused' concepts (like the 'ether' in physics), which are meaningless and useless? Gallie's answer is that the 'essentially contested' differs from the 'radically confused' in two principal ways: first, there is an 'original exemplar' – we must once have known what the thing was – and second, that contesting the meaning leads to 'progress'. This must mean that we are intellectually better off in some general sense; it cannot mean progress towards an agreed definition. Ultimately, the case is not proven: I think that there is at least as strong a case for saying that art is radically confused. But either will do for my main argument, since there can be no doubt that radically confused, as well as essentially contested, concepts can have good and bad effects on people's lives.

The first major indictment of art is that it detracts from life. I mean here the practice of art understood by its practitioners in the context of the concept of art, with all its attendant aspirations. The person who is trying to photograph the Valley of the Kings at dawn should be enjoying the moment (including the crowds, since they are there anyway). The world would be better off if most of the people writing poems for the BBC 'find a poet' competition spent the time playing with their children – or playing pushpin, if that would give them more pleasure. For a utilitarian, the richest and most important thing in life is sensation. The feeling of exhausted exhilaration when you get to the top with two of your sons and simultaneously feel the warm west wind and see the view. Dancing and jumping with that old man when Brian O'Neill scored against United in 1968. The soft cheek of a tiny, new-born relative. The winter sun picking out the rocks on Cleeve Hill as your horse comes up the slope to win at 6–1. Sharing the taste of the first cutting of asparagus from the garden. Meaningful, shared pleasures. And I haven't even mentioned love!

There is an account of the good life as essentially sensual in William Morris's 'Utopian' novel, *News from Nowhere*.[45] The date is roughly 2050 (as seen from 1890), and the post-revolutionary population of England is spread out among the stately homes, living in communes. In one sense, there is no art; in another, art is everywhere and everything. But it is essentially *craft*, without intellectual or spiritual significance. It is the sights and textures that delight, but these are usually the sensual concomitant of some simple human function: the well-grown vegetable and the well-crafted belt. It is the opposite of Le Corbusier's world, because decoration is every-where and is intrinsic to goodness. But Morris is, of course, a Marxist (of sorts) and envisages the sensuous life as only being possible after a revolution that has swept away existing institutions and 'hang-ups' (as they would later be called, though he clearly has the concept without the phrase). I, on the other hand, do not envisage such a change, and would not like it if it happened; more in the spirit of Morris's contem-porary, Samuel Smiles, I am recommending that we remake our own lives in this way.

The other great reason to indict art is that it offers a false pretension, which diverts human beings from their highest and best capacity and activity – reason and philosophy, respectively. Sentience is shared by both the ploughman and his mouse-victim, but only the ploughman can make sense of it. The most wonderful and beautiful and satisfying of human aspirations are philosophical in the broader sense, including physics and mathematics; this is the unique realm of the profound and the true. But, given Pareto's pyramid, most people cannot even face the nature of such inquiry, and find a kind of mock profundity in the arts. As a society, we are obsessed with the arts. As so often, I can rely on Dr Theodore Dalrymple to state the exact opposite of the case:

> The English are not, on the whole, interested in modern art or indeed art of any description.[46]

There is, admittedly, an ambiguity here, because the essay quoted is specifically about the visual arts; but it is philosophy about which the English really know nothing. They are quite artistic in the broader sense, and read more than ten times as many novels as the Italians (I agree with the Italians, for what it's worth). One horrific piece of information, which actually made me 'shudder and turn away' (the phrase comes from Hugh Dalton's description of G. D. H. Cole coming across the actual working class, rather than the one he had imagined for his own purposes), was that in Radio 4's 2005 poll about the greatest ever philosopher, Karl Marx came top with 28 per cent of the vote.[47] *Karl Marx!* – a crashing old bore with tyrannical tendencies, who was wrong every time he was clear enough to be judged right or wrong! But worse than that – Karl Marx's 'philosophy' was the equivalent of Tracey Emin's bed, a kind of anti-philosophy. He wrote *The Poverty of Philosophy*, for heaven's sake, which helped a disastrously successful post-philosophical movement to replace philosophy with a kind of covertly moralistic socio-economic contextualising.

My fear here is not that Radio 4 listeners, who are a pretty fair sample of the educated middle classes in England, are covert Marxists. It is that they are so ignorant that they cannot name a philosopher, and certainly don't have a favourite one. So they name Marx; they have heard of him, because he was historically important. Which I find very sad, because reading David Hume was the most exciting thing that ever happened to me, intellectually speaking. And I blame the arts and their status in a system of education that makes adolescents read dreary novels instead of books that actually say something. Artistic expressions offer feelings of profundity, but not the real thing; a sense of intellectual importance without the reality. On a slightly more cheerful note, Hume did come second in the poll, having been promoted strongly by the *Economist* magazine.

I should make clear that my objections are to the concept and status of 'art' and 'the arts', not to the practice. I have no wish to censor anything, and I (just about) accept a public goods argument for subsidising some of 'the arts', where there is a specific case and not just because they are 'the arts'. I am a fairly enthusiastic consumer of most of them, including painting, music and, especially, theatre. So the question arises: what do I think I get out of them?

Quite a lot, I think, is extrinsic to the 'art' involved. I have several times attended courses at the National Gallery in London and listened to lectures on particular paintings. These are partly about technique, but mostly about context and purpose. Thus you can look at Hans Holbein's *The Ambassadors* and see detailed implications and meaning even in the belts the two men are wearing, let alone in the curious object at their feet, which is a clearly drawn skull – but only from one angle. It is fascinating as an insight into a period; but it is the detail that fascinates, and that has nothing to do with art. A collection of menus and restaurant bills from the same period, fully explained and contextualised, would be equally interesting.

I have been to hundreds of productions of Shakespeare plays. Why? After a good production I feel uplifted all next day. In a recent review of all three parts of *Henry VI*, seen on a single day, I tried to ask myself why I felt so good after ten hours of slaughter, hatred and betrayal.[48] I was certainly no nearer to understanding whether God exists, or what it would mean to say the universe is infinite, or whether there is such a thing as natural law. But I had been taken out of myself, into another world created by the author, the director and the actors. It was, above all, a world in which they spoke a more beautiful language, generally comprehensible, sometimes stretching comprehension, emotionally involving, but allowing safe return. It was much more than mere 'entertainment', but it was not philosophical investigation either. I'm sorry to labour this point, but there are those who think that Shakespeare is of *intellectual* significance, and that studying his works is some kind of equivalent or substitute for studying Hobbes and Hume. By a happy freak of my education, I never did study him, but I did act Shakespeare, and gained great sensual pleasure from just saying his words.

Thus 'the arts' can offer us sensuous passion and gratify our love of detail. Music, in my view, is all passion. It is intellectually enormously complicated, and its complexity has mathematical precision: I have always been fascinated by the way in which a combination of tone, key and phrasing can manipulate emotion. But understanding that does nothing one way or another to the sensuous pleasure and the emotion.

Enjoy the art. Love the artist. But do not respect the artist – especially if he calls himself by that title.

10

'OTHERS': CULTURES AND BOUNDARIES

I spent my childhood and youth in North Lancashire and my late twenties in Northern California. The two are as different as two places could be that nominally speak the same language, and a good deal of understanding – as well as humour – can be extracted from a comparison.

Attitudes to health are a case in point. In a rain-swept Pennine town you meet Albert, who has just struggled up the cobbled street and is resting from the exertion, wheezing audibly, before he makes his final assault on the steps of the Dog and Partridge. 'How are you, Albert?' you ask. 'Grand', he replies. Far away, in the foothills of the Santa Cruz mountains, Kevin has just come off the tennis court and is sipping an orange juice by the pool. He is six foot three inches tall, his skin is golden brown and his teeth are so white and straight that, if you spotted them back in Lancashire, you would assume they were made in a factory. 'How are you, Kevin?' you ask, and a tale of three shrinks and two allergies is unfolded. Or was it two shrinks and three allergies?

The particular cultural divide that affected me was really about rudeness – or frankness. Behaviour that was normal to me was considered 'excessively critical' or 'judgemental'. That is, in the more recent sense of 'judgemental': 'inclined to make judgements, especially moral or personal ones'. Actually, I think I was probably relatively innocent of the accusation of judgementalism, because my judgements were relatively few and relatively benign; but I did articulate them. By contrast, I can think of check-out clerks at my local Alpha Beta supermarket when they were presented with food stamps as payment by young men with waist-length hair. Their whole bodies would seethe with judgement, but they were allowed to say nothing.

I was probably more genuinely guilty of excessive criticism in the academic context. The local sub-culture seemed to me to be so excessively respectful and polite as to be dysfunctional when measured in terms of intellectual progress – or even the individual progress of those in need of criticism. It was my assumption that the overwhelming bulk of academic work (at least 90 per cent) was either unoriginal or fundamentally flawed; this contrasted with the local public assumption that pretty well everything could be called a 'valuable contribution'.

In theoretical terms, there are both sociological and philosophical angles from which this cultural difference can be seen. The sociology of it falls under the theory of Imperial Eggshells: that is to say, in empires that contain numerous and contested identities, it is functional, at least on a day-to-day basis, to develop codes and boundaries, which remove the threats those identities pose to one another. There was no such need in the Lancashire of my childhood; it was a relatively homogeneous place, and if you didn't like a group of people you said so fairly often: Labour supporters and Roman Catholics were the most stigmatised groups in the Tory and Anglican circles I moved in. It was then customary to add that X, who was a member of one of these groups but whom you happened to know, was a splendid chap and did not fall into the normal pattern.

In more diverse societies, there was a great deal more restraint about how you talked about groups: these included British India, the Austro-Hungarian Empire and the USA. By way of experiment, I recently flew from South Africa, where people treated each other as though they were all walking on eggshells, to Australia, where aboriginals hurled abuse at 'white' people and (to a lesser extent) vice versa. There must be considerable doubt whether codes which silence antipathies do anything to reduce them: look what happened to British India and the Austro-Hungarian Empire. Also look at what happened in Bosnia, remembering that most western journalists covering the Sarajevo Winter Olympics in 1984 observed it to be a fine example of peaceful multiculturalism.

The question that arises in political philosophy is whether such 'politenesses' should be enforced, particularly by the state. Enforcement, in this context, refers primarily to legislation, but must also be taken to include the use of state agencies, such as the BBC and the education system, to foster forms of political correctness. For a utilitarian, there is a *prima facie* case on both sides. The 'thin end of the wedge' argument suggests that insults open the way to greater cruelties, so that criminalising certain kinds of insult and private discrimination may help protect us against violent inter-communal conflict. I would nervously concede that race relations legislation may have had net benefit effects in this way. The nervousness stems not simply from the fact that such legislation forms the thin end of another wedge – assault on free speech – but also from the fact that it tends to be abused, in that the concept of 'race' becomes extended. That is, there is a very strong case for protecting people from racial criticism in the strictly biological sense. The point is not that such attacks are misconceived because there are no ethically significant differences between races; that is true (I believe), but free speech must apply to false and absurd propositions, as well as to true ones. Rather, the thing is that nobody can choose their race in the biological sense. Crudely, nothing is lost if we ban people from saying that black skin is not as good as white skin, because there is no good that can come of such statements. But if 'race' is extended, as it has been, to include 'ethnicity', and if 'ethnicity' is then taken to include religion, we rapidly reach the point at which we cannot criticise 'halal' butchery in a country in which some people are so concerned about animal welfare that fox hunting is illegal.

The case for free speech has, as its minor theme, the opposite argument to the 'thin end of the wedge' – the 'safety valve' argument. If the Jews are believed to be poisoning the wells, this should be stated publicly as early as possible, so that we can examine the evidence. The well-poisoning theory should not be left to rumour, or only invoked in times of social breakdown or high emotion. Nobody should be allowed to assert it as if it were something that has so far been deliberately concealed. It is surely easier to tolerate those you do not have to respect than it is to put up with those who require deference from you. Which is yet another aspect of the Hanoverian Solution, and the key to understanding how monarchy and aristocracy managed to survive in England, but not, for the most part, on the Continent.

But the major argument for free speech stems from our interest in the truth, and our necessary and humble recognition that we know very little. The 'classic' liberal case for free speech, as put by John Stuart Mill, does not arise out of any 'right' to express yourself, and wholly pre-empts any supposition of group rights and the possible clash with individual rights. It depends solely on the utility of debate in seeking the truth, which is to say in eradicating some fraction of the colossal errors to which mankind has normally been subjected. Free speech, as justified by this argument, cannot be polite and gentle. It must be limitless in principle (though, of course, it may be limited in certain forms and contexts; that is no longer much of a problem, given the range of forms of expression available). It must be robust in style and call nonsense nonsense; respect and compromise do not serve the highest purposes of free speech, but venom and scorn do. And it must be individual, allowing a single person to be heard. In Mill's version, freedom of speech is not for bullies and the picket-line – it is for the individual non-conformist who will not accept the orthodoxy; the boy who is prepared to say that the Emperor is naked.[49]

The greatest enemies of the vigorous debate and acerbic scepticism recommended by the essay 'On Liberty' have been those most threatened by it – priests, mullahs and scientific socialists. But governments are never truly sympathetic to the cause of free expression, and find new reasons for curtailing it in every generation. The cause of civil peace in a 'multicultural' society is probably the principal current threat, and its worst expression in the United Kingdom is the Racial and

Religious Hatred Act 2006.[50] This was much 'watered down' during a turbulent debate. If it really is concerned with 'hatred' (which is not a nice thing), it is closer to being acceptable than it was originally, and it has been made clear that scorn is not hatred. In fact, in lieu of any case law for the moment, it seems likely that, to fall foul of this law, your words would have to be intended to stimulate violent action (such as arson against a mosque) and to succeed in doing so: only the Attorney General can initiate a prosecution. But the Act does, in principle, cross yet another line in the erosion of free speech, and we are offered no guarantees as to who might become Attorney General. If the mullah wants to say that I am evil and will go to hell, then he should say so without let or hindrance. And if I want to say that his religion is a castle built on sand, that it has been the chief agent of immiseration in the world, and that it ought to be dumped in the dustbin of history, then I ought to say so. Scorn for opinion does not imply hatred of persons: some of my best friends believe arrant nonsense.

In a similar spirit to this legislation is Prince Charles' assertion in a 1994 television interview that he might change the title of 'Defender of the Faith', acquired by Henry VIII in his Roman phase, to 'Defender of Faith', to acknowledge the 'multi-faith' nature of his future subjects. To which one should respond that the title, as it came to designate the duties of the head of the Anglican Church, was appreciated by many as a defence against all other (more dogmatic and more authoritarian) faiths, particularly against Roman Catholicism, though Catholicism only had this priority because we didn't seem to need a defender against Islam. If there were to be a publicly sponsored 'Defender of Faith', there should also be a well-funded, well-staffed office of the 'Attacker of Faith'. I am currently available.

An extension of the threat to free speech – and also to the principle of utilitarianism – lies in the remaining 'Westphalian system' of separate states. For all the current talk in academic international studies of globalisation and of the development of regimes and systems of government that are not dependent on states and not limited by state boundaries, the political and legal world still consists, *prima facie*, of states that demonstrate a built-in enthusiasm for the defence of sovereignty. This is a rule of respect in the formal sense: we start with the assumption that what goes on beyond our boundaries is not our business. It is a good rule insofar as it renders us free from responsibility – we are happier not having to bear responsibility for Africa. And it is a bad rule for exactly the same reason: if Africa had remained part of European-based empires in a developing global system for at least another 50 years, it would surely not have been allowed to suffer so badly as it has done. The system of respect for sovereignty is only good in a *prima facie* sort of way. Formal respect does not imply moral respect: we can acknowledge your borders without thinking you have any virtue. And it must have limits for a utilitarian – there must be levels of misery and cruelty at which we conclude that the sovereignty rule is not working and that we should invade, if we have the capacity. It is notable that tyrannies, like Saudi Arabia and the People's Republic of China, are the most prominent not only in insisting on the sovereignty rule, but in wanting to extend it to prohibit 'insults'.

11

DISSING RESPECT – A SUMMARY

Gangsters and governments, rat-boys and rascals all demand our respect. Their demands are not clear or conceptually coherent, and they are also, taken together, the symptoms of a profound intellectual and ethical malaise. The historic nature of the malaise is a failure to develop the great philosophical insights of the 18th century. Instead of becoming more free, more rational and more happy, as it appeared we were becoming, we have groped back to the old neediness for wholenesses and onenesses and absolute and intrinsic values, resuscitating the old mental tyrannies of religion under the name of humanism. Ten Commandments or Human Rights: both require an abnegation of our capacity to calculate consequences and choose the best result.

'Respect' has many different connotations and nuances, but its proper use can be reduced to two meanings. They are a careful acknowledgement of a legitimately acquired right, or a spontaneous admiration of virtue. Respect is often too much to ask of other people: why should they admire you when their ideas of worth are different from yours? But it is also too little: why be satisfied with the cold collation of respect, when the warmer dishes of charm, affection and friendship might be available? When people need to be respected, that very need makes them unworthy of respect. When you are asked to respect intellectual or artistic effort or cultural identity *a priori,* you should keep an open mind, emphasising your right to be contemptuous and the probability of your exercising that right. When governments try to paper over the gaps in the social fabric by calling for norms of respect, tell them that the cracks should be seen, understood and accepted.

I am not here proposing the Respect (Lack of) Act 2008. This is not a case for legislation, though some minor repeals would be good. Rather, this essay is intended to play a small part in the kind of shifting of opinion away from nonsense that, in the past, brought about such diverse events as the Restoration, the Permissive Society and the fall of the Soviet Union.

NOTES

PROLEGOMENON

1 W. R. 'Dean' Inge, *England*, 3rd edition, Benn, 1926, p. 65.

SAY WHAT YOU'RE GOING TO SAY ... AND WHY

2 Theodore Dalrymple, 'It is the inescapable duty of every decent citizen to express no interest or enthusiasm for football and the World Cup', at www.socialaffairsunit.org.uk/blog/archives/000966.php (posted 7 June 2006).

3 See, for example: www.respect.gov.uk/content.aspx?id=7524; www.number10.gov.uk/output/Page8898.asp

4 See http://news.bbc.co.uk/1/hi/uk_politics/4554179.stm

5 John Dickie, *Cosa Nostra: A History of the Sicilian Mafia*, Coronet, 2007.

6 Quoted in John Miller, *Peter Ustinov, The Gift of Laughter: The Authorised Biography*, Weidenfeld & Nicolson, 2002, pp. 207–8.

7 Samuel Smiles, *Self-Help, with illustrations of conduct and perseverance*, Centenary Edition, John Murray, 1958, p. 35 (first published 1859).

8 Jeremy Bentham, 'Anarchical Fallacies', available at http://jan.ucc.nau.edu/~dss4/bentham1.pdf; 'Of Torture' is in the Bentham Manuscripts, University College, London, 46/63–70.

9 Robert Goodin, 'Government House utilitarianism'. In Lincoln Allison (ed.), *The Utilitarian Response: The Contemporary Viability of Utilitarian Political Philosophy*, Sage, 1990, pp. 140–60.

THREE HISTORICAL REFLECTIONS

10 David Hume, *The History of England*, Vol. VI, Liberty Classics (Indianapolis), 1983, based on the 1778 edition, p. 531.

11 David Hume, 'Of the Protestant succession', in *Essays Moral, Political and Literary*, Liberty Classics (Indianapolis), 1985, based on

Vol. 1 of the 1777 *Essays and Treatises on Several Subjects*, pp. 504–5.

12 Hume, *History*, p. 532.

13 *Ibid*., p. 533.

14 Hume, 'Of the middle station in life', *Essays*, p. 551.

15 Voltaire, '*Sur les Presbyteriens*', in *Lettres sur les Anglais*, Pitt, 1931, p. 21. Full English text available at www.fordham.edu/halsall/mod/1778voltaire-lettres.html

16 Sir Arthur Bryant, 'The years of disillusion', in *The Age of Elegance*, Reprint Society, 1954, pp. 348–98.

17 Samuel Smiles, *Self-Help, with Illustrations of Conduct and Perseverance*, Centenary Edition, John Murray, 1958, p. 290.

18 Thorstein Veblen, *The Theory of the Leisure Class: An Economic Study of Institutions*, Allen & Unwin, 1925.

19 Vance Packard, *The Status Seekers: An Explanation of Class Behavior in America and the Hidden Barriers That Affect You, Your Community, Your Future*, McKay (New York), 1959.

20 Fred Hirsch, *Social Limits to Growth*, Harvard University Press, 1976.

21 F. M. L. Thompson, *The Rise of Respectable Society, A Social History of Victorian Britain, 1830–1900*, Fontana, 1988.

22 Lytton Strachey, *Eminent Victorians*, with an Introduction by Michael Holroyd, Penguin, 1986.

23 This song became quite well known and was sung by football fans to 'wind up' the police well into the 1970s. Harry Roberts was referred to in several songs by the 'punk anarchist' band Chumbawamba, and appears as a thinly disguised Billy Porter in Jake Arnott's novel *He Kills Coppers*, published by Hodder & Stoughton in 2001. At the time of writing, the man himself, who should have been executed in the 1960s, is still alive; he was refused parole in September 2006.

24 I was offered a place by University College, Oxford, at the age of 16, but had to find something to do until they would allow me to 'go up' more than a year later.

25 See interview with Peter Shaw, manager of the Whitbread hop farm in Lincoln Allison, 'Once there were Sevenoaks', *The Countryman*, Vol. 95, No. 5, Dec.–Jan., 1990–91.

26 *As You Like* It, Act II, Scene 1, lines 3–4.

27 Matthew Arnold, *Culture and Anarchy and Other Writings*, Cambridge University Press, 1993, p. 70 (*Culture and Anarchy*, first published 1869).

28 Bernard Darwin, *W. G. Grace*, Duckworth, 1934; C. L. R. James, *Beyond a Boundary*, Stanley Paul, 1963, esp. pp. 157–83.

DO NOT HONOUR THY FATHER AND THY MOTHER

29 Samuel Butler, *Erewhon*, Penguin Books, 1936 (first published 1872).

A DISRESPECTFUL EDUCATION

30 Francis Gilbert, *Yob Nation*, Portrait Books, 2006, p. 278.
31 Fred Hirsch, *Social Limits to Growth*, Harvard University Press, 1976.

RESPECT FOR HUMANS, ANIMALS ... EVEN OIKS?

32 In Ronald Dworkin, *Taking Rights Seriously*, Harvard University Press, 1977.
33 Jeremy Bentham, 'Anarchical Fallacies', available at http://jan.ucc.nau.edu/~dss4/bentham1.pdf
34 Robert Burns, 'To a Mouse', in *Poetical Works*, ed. William Wallace, Chambers, 1990, p. 73.
35 Edward C. Banfield (with Laura Fasano), *The Moral Basis of a Backward Society*, The Free Press (Glencoe), 1958; Edward C. Banfield, *The Unheavenly City, the Nature and Future of our Urban Crisis*, Little, Brown (Boston), 1968.
36 Theodore Dalrymple, *Our Culture: What's Left of It, The Mandarins and the Masses*, Ivan R. Dee (Chicago), 2005.
37 John Donne's writings can be accessed at www.luminarium.org/sevenlit/donne/donnebib.htm
38 Patrick Devlin, *The Enforcement of Morals*, Oxford University Press, 1965.

PSYCHOWANNABES

39 Harold D. Lasswell, *Psychopathology and Politics with Afterthoughts by the Author*, Viking Press, 1960 (first published 1930).
40 James Lees-Milne, *Diaries, 1942–54*, abridged and introduced by Michael Bloch, John Murray, 2006, p. 171 (first published 1975).
41 http://movies.uk.msn.com/features/CringyOscarSpeeches_gallery.aspx?imageindex=2#2980245
42 Walter Bagehot, *The English Constitution*, 2nd edition, first published 1873. Available at http://socserv2.mcmaster.ca/~econ/ugcm/3ll3/bagehot/constitution.pdf

43 J. A. Schumpeter, *Capitalism, Socialism and Democracy*, Allen and Unwin, 1976, Part 4 (first published 1942).

RESPECT FOR THE ARTIST

44 W. B. Gallie, 'Essentially Contested Concepts', *Proceedings of the Aristotelian Society*, Vol. LVI, 1955–56.

45 William Morris, *News from Nowhere or An Epoch of Rest, Being Some Chapters from a Utopian Romance* (first published 1890). Available at www.marxists.org/archive/morris/works/1890/nowhere/nowhere.htm

46 Theodore Dalrymple, *Our Culture: What's Left of It, The Mandarins and the Masses*, Ivan R. Dee (Chicago), 2005, p. 140.

47 See Mark Seldon, 'Kapital Gains', *Guardian*, 14 July 2005.

48 Lincoln Allison, 'The Terrors of the Bear-Garden' at www.socialaffairsunit.org.uk/blog/archives/001204.php

'OTHERS': CULTURES AND BOUNDARIES

49 Hans Christian Andersen's allegorical story quite rightly ranks with Conan Doyle's non-barking dog among the favourite literary references of academics. It was invented, not collected, by Andersen and first published in 1837, whereas 'On Liberty' was first published in 1859. So far as I know, Mill was not aware of the story.

50 See www.publications.parliament.uk/pa/cm200506/cmbills/011/06011.i-i.html and http://news.bbc.co.uk/1/hi/uk/3873323.stm